"REALLY"
Quick and Easy

"A Collection of
Delicious-Easy-to-Prepare Recipes"

From the Kitchen of
Shirley Heston

Judy Morehead Photography
Lancaster, Ohio 43130

G&R
Publishing Co.

507 Industrial Street
Waverly, IA 50677
1-800-383-1679

#6261

Dedication

I am dedicating this book to all women and men who love to cook but have very little time to do so. The joy of cooking for your family, friends and for yourself can be fun when you use these Quick & Easy recipes that I have compiled in this book. I have included 30 days of Sample Menus for your convenience. This should help you when you are trying to decide what to have for "DINNER"! These recipes take ingredients that you usually have on hand and the cost to buy them is very inexpensive.

I also want to dedicate this book to all of my friends at <u>Fairfield</u> <u>National</u> <u>Bank</u> and <u>Fairfield</u> <u>County</u> <u>Clerk</u> of <u>Courts</u> office in Lancaster. They have been avid supporters of my first cookbook, "Cookin In Fairfield County" and I hope that they will enjoy this one as well.

Today, almost everyone has a very busy schedule and my wish is that all who purchase this cookbook will enjoy the collection of recipes and the ease of preparing them.

"Happy Cookin' and God Bless;"

Shirley Heston

Shirley Heston

Something About The Author

I was born in Lancaster, Ohio. Our town is located in the beautiful rolling hills of Fairfield County in southeastern Ohio. I was raised on a farm and learned to do most of the farm chores including milking and plowing the fields, besides learning to cook. My parents are Edgar and Hattie Kull. My dad passed away in 1964 and my Mom is still living and STILL cooks delicious meals. I have two sisters and one brother. I am married to Jim Heston and have four children and 10 grandchildren. My family consists of son, Dave and wife Heidi, their children, Aimee and Anna; son, Don and wife, Joyce, their children, Ryan, Chris, Misty, and Joshua; daughter, Charlotte and husband, John Cofman, their children, Andy, Jenna, and John Paul; and daughter Debbie.

My husband, Jim, and I own and operate Heston's Auto Service and Used Cars in Lancaster, Ohio. This year we are celebrating our 53rd year of being in business and our 41st year of marriage.

I love music and enjoy being the music director at Emanuel Lutheran Church in Lancaster. I like to enter cooking and baking contests and have been fortunate to have won several prizes and have had some of my recipes published in magazines. I love cooking and my favorite time is when I cook for my family and friends. Each month I have a "Birthday Party" at our house and honor the family members who are having a birthday that month. This is one of my ways of showing my love for my family and friends. This also gives everyone a chance to visit. I always try to prepare some of their favorite foods and make their favorite birthday cake.

I enjoy writing cookbooks and hope all that buy this cookbook enjoy using it and enjoy the ease of preparing good meals for their families.

"Happy Cooking and May God Bless"

Shirley Heston

Sel Gris

"Gray salt" is harvested on France's Atlantic coast where shallow basins are flooded with ocean water. Evaporation takes place between May and September when artisan harvesters rake the salt to the edge of each bed. The salt picks up its gray color and distinct flavor from minerals in the bed's clay bottom.

Fleur de Sel

A finishing salt that I think is worth its high price tag. A by-product of sel gris, fleur de sel is created only when the winds are calm and the days are warm. It is on these rare few days that the gray salt "blooms" lacy, white crystals. This is the "flower of salt" and is carefully skimmed from the surface. Use sparingly on foods just before serving.

am I telling you this? It's the design that makes kosher salt so good. This structure dissolves easily and imparts plenty of flavor (without oversalting) because of its large surface area. We use it in our test kitchen.

Red Alae Hawaiian Sea Salt

Hawaiian red and black sea salts (black not shown) are specialty finishing salts. While they look cool, their flavor is a bit strange. Red salt has an iron taste from the soil that's used to add color, while the black salt tends to have a sulfuric aroma from added purified lava.

making crème fraîche

Many recipes call for crème fraîche, a thick, tangy French cream similar to sour cream, but smoother and richer. Its body and thickness comes from natural bacteria in unpasteurized cream. But since this is an unpasteurized process, we have to improvise in the States by using the natural fermenting agents in buttermilk. Mix 1 cup heavy cream, ¼ cup buttermilk, and 1 tablespoon lemon juice. Cover and let sit at room temperature 6–8 hours, then refrigerate. Crème fraîche is great for cooking because of its rich flavor and stability—it doesn't break when heated, unlike sour cream.

▲ *Add buttermilk and lemon juice to cream. Let sit at room temperature, then chill. Use when thick.*

clarifying butter

Clarifying butter is a process used to separate the milk solids from the oily butterfat in butter. You've probably experienced putting whole butter into a hot pan—it quickly turns brown. That browning is the milk solids cooking. They just can't tolerate higher heats.

To get the butter taste without the browning, clarify butter. Slowly melt whole butter over low heat. You'll eventually see three layers form. The top layer is foamy and made up of water and milk—skim it off and discard. The deep yellow middle layer is the butterfat—pour this off into a container. This is the clarified butter you want to use for sauteing. What's left in the bottom are the milk solids—pitch them.

What to use

At $30 a pound, you need to exercise good judgment when selecting salts for your kitchen—especially exotic salts.

For regular cooking, nothing beats 70¢ a pound kosher salt. It blends well, is clean-tasting, easy to cook with, and additive free. All of the qualities of expensive salts get lost during cooking. Their value is geared towards finished food—that is, sprinkling on top of food just before serving. Texture as well as taste become important for a finishing salt.

My favorites, hands down, are fleur de sel and Maldon sea salts. Their flavors are mild and textures pleasingly crisp.

Maldon Sea Salt

Besides fleur de sel, England's Maldon sea salt is worth its $11 a pound price. This is a good "finishing salt" that gets its delicate flavor from a tradition of boiling the sea water to form hollow, pyramid-shaped crystals. You can actually crush the crystals between your fingers. This makes for a light taste on your tongue.

Table Salt

Except for baking, I haven't used table salt in years. It always seems to taste really salty and harsh. The reality is that it isn't any saltier than other salts, it's just that the crystals are small and don't dissolve well. Because of this, the crystals tend to linger on the surface of the tongue.

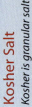

Kosher Salt

Kosher is granular salt that's pressed together. If you look at it micro-

At last a cookbook that REALLY has Quick and Easy recipes to prepare for your family. The ease of preparation and length of time to prepare are the wonderful things this cookbook has to offer.

The recipes use ingredients that you usually have in your cupboard and are very inexpensive to purchase, I have put together a group of Sample Menus to help you decide quickly what to prepare for your family.

Sample Breakfast Menu

Apple Cinnamon Rolls pg. 44	Cinnamon Sticks pg. 7
Fruit Juice and Coffee	Fried Apples pg. 35
	Fruit Juice and Coffee
English Egg Muffins pg. 8	Biscuit Monkey Bread pg. 8
Fruit Juice and Coffee	Fruit Juice and Coffee
Fresh Fruit With Dip pg. 45	
Apple Pancakes pg. 9	Seven-Up Pancakes pg. 9
Syrup of your choice	Syrup of your choice
Fruit Juice and Coffee	Fruit Juice and Coffee
Oven-Baked French Toast pg. 10	Apple Breakfast Pie pg. 10
Syrup of your choice	Fruit Juice and Coffee
Fruit Juice and Coffee	

Sample Lunch Menu

Egg Salad Filling Served on Croissants pg. 51	Scrambled Eggs and Chicken pg. 12
Microwave S'mores pg. 42	Fruit Cookie Pizza pg. 42
Hot Ham and Cheese Sandwiches pg. 52	Vegetable Pasta pg. 50
Candy Bar Pie pg. 31	Choco-Peanut Butter Mounds pg. 33
Mexican Chicken & Cheese Sandwich pg. 52	Chicken Salad (Quick & Easy) pg. 29
Baked Pineapple Casserole pg. 36	Fried Apples pg. 35
	Easy Muffins pg. 5

Sample Dinner Menu

Yummy Apricot Chicken pg. 11 Broccoli Casserole pg. 50 Quick Biscuits pg. 6 Yogurt Pie pg. 33	Quick Chicken Casserole pg. 16 Yummy Potato Slices pg. 47 Quick Chocolate Mousse pg. 35	Chicken Biscuit Cups pg. 16 Potato Patties pg. 48 Very Easy Chocolate Cake pg. 39
Easy Chicken & Noodles pg. 11 Potato Patties pg. 48 Easy Muffins pg. 5 Very Easy Peach Cobbler pg. 40	Oven Fried Mustard Chicken pg. 14 Herb Roasted Potatoes pg. 48 Easy Muffins pg. 5 Lemonade Stand Pie pg. 31	Quick and Easy Chicken Cordon Bleu pg. 16 Broccoli Casserole pg. 50 Quick Breadsticks pg. 5 Quick Blender Cherry Pie pg. 31
Super Chicken Casserole pg. 11 Green Bean Casserole pg. 49 Blueberry Ice Cream Muffins pg. 7 Fresh Fruit With Fruit Dip pg. 45	Easy Chicken Pasta pg. 14 Parmesan Biscuits pg. 6 Apple Crunch pg. 36	Chicken Italiano pg. 16 Yummy Potato Oven Slices pg. 47 Toasty Bread Snacks pg. 6 Fresh Fruit With Fruit Dip pg. 45
Shirley's Baked Chicken pg. 12 Quick Rice Pudding pg. 36 Parmesan Biscuits pg. 6	Favorite Chicken Pot Pie pg. 14 Tossed Salad With Blue Cheese Dressing pg. 29 Peach Crisp pg. 41	Escalloped Chicken pg. 17 Green Bean Casserole pg. 49 Low Fat Brownies pg. 43
Chicken Pockets pg. 12 Cream of Broccoli Soup pg. 27 Yogurt Pie pg. 33	Zesty Chicken Italian pg. 15 Vegetable Pasta pg. 50 Parmesan Biscuits pg. 6 Little Fruit Tarts pg. 34	Turkey or Chicken Super Supper pg. 17 Herb Roasted Potatoes pg. 48 Easy Muffins pg. 5 Very Easy Cheesecake pg. 39
Chinese Chicken pg. 13 Crescents Almond Rolls pg. 7 Quick and Easy Key Lime Pie pg. 33	Chicken Stuffing Casserole pg. 15 Tossed Salad With Quick French Dressing pg. 30 Toasty Bread Snacks pg. 6 Jiffy Peanut Butter Pie pg. 32	Easy Chicken and Vegetable Stir-Fry pg. 17 Quick Rice Pudding pg. 36 Crescent Almond Rolls pg. 7
Parmesan Chicken pg. 13 Impossible Broccoli Pie pg. 47 Quick Breadsticks pg. 5 Peach Bread Pudding pg. 41	Chicken Broccoli Casserole pg. 15 Quick Rice Pudding pg. 36 Herb Biscuits pg. 5	Quick Chicken and Broccoli Pie pg. 18 No-Fry French Fries pg. 49 Quick Breadsticks pg. 5 Pecan Dessert pg. 37

Sample Dinner Menu

Good and Easy Taco Pie pg. 18
Green Bean Casserole pg. 49
Easy Lemon Tarts pg. 34
	Easy Spaghetti Pie pg. 21
	Fried Apples pg. 35
	Parmesan Cheese Biscuits pg. 6
		Microwave Sweet and Sour
		   Meatballs pg. 23
		Microwave Sautéed
		   Mushrooms pg. 51
		Toasty Bread Snacks pg. 6
		Creamy Cherry Dessert pg. 34

Quick and Easy Beef Hash pg. 19 Quick Biscuits pg. 6 Lemonade Stand Pie pg. 31	Sloppy Joes pg. 21 Quick Vegetable Soup pg. 27 Very Easy Peach Cobbler pg. 40	Tuna Burgers pg. 24 Quick Vegetable Soup pg. 27 Little Fruit Tarts pg. 34

Crunchy Onion Burgers pg. 19
Easy Skillet Baked Beans pg. 47
Twinkie Surprise pg. 38
	Hamburger Spread
	   Sandwich pg. 21
	Quick and Yummy Corn
	   Chowder pg. 27
	Twinkie Surprise pg. 38
		Best Ever Tuna Casserole pg. 24
		Herb Biscuits pg. 5
		Supreme Blueberry
		   Cobbler pg. 41

Beef Chili Macaroni pg. 19 Parmesan Biscuits pg. 6 Heavenly Fruit Dessert pg. 37	Easy Cheeseburger Pie pg. 22 Toasty Bread Snacks pg. 6 Lemon Delight pg. 37	Delicious Easy Flounder Au Gratin pg. 24 Cheesy Vegetables pg. 48 Beer Buns pg. 6 Upside Down Cherry Pie pg. 32
Shirley's White Castles pg. 20 No Fry French Fries pg. 49 Quick One Bowl Brownies pg. 42	Quick and Easy Lasagna Pie pg. 22 Quick Bread Sticks pg. 5 Cottage Cheese Dessert pg. 38	Beer Batter Fish pg. 25 No Fry Oven Fries pg. 49 Parmesan Biscuits pg. 6 Fried Apples pg. 35

Cheeseburger Macaroni pg. 20
Toasty Bread Snacks pg. 6
Upside Down Cherry Pie pg. 32
	Best Crock Pot Chili pg. 23
	Crackers
	Quick and Easy Fruit
	   Turnovers pg. 39
		Hot Ham and Cheese
		   Sandwiches pg. 52
		Ham and Potato Soup pg. 28
		Quick Ice Cream Pie pg. 32

Quick Vegetables and Beef pg. 20
Corn Fritters pg. 51
Quick Bread Sticks pg. 5
	Beef Oven Porcupines pg. 23
	Green Bean Casserole pg. 49
	Easy Muffins pg. 5
	Quick and Easy Cherry
	   Cobbler pg. 40
		Mexican Chicken and
		   Cheese Sandwich pg. 52
		Broccoli Casserole pg. 50
		Quick Cinnamon Apple
		   Cake pg. 38

Suggested Groceries To Keep On Hand

It is impossible to have all ingredients for all recipes; but these are some of the most used staples to have on hand.

Canned chicken, I prefer white meat
Canned tuna, I like tuna pack in
 water
Canned chicken broth
Canned pie fillings
Canned fruits
Canned vegetables
Canned kidney beans and baked
 beans
Canned chopped or whole
 tomatoes
Canned tomato juice
Canned tomato paste
Canned tomato sauce
Canned mushrooms
Frozen chicken breasts, I buy the
 individual frozen, skinless and
 boneless
Frozen noodles
Frozen dinner rolls, ready-to-bake
Frozen vegetables
Refrigerated biscuits
Refrigerated crescent rolls
Margarine sticks
Crisco shortening
Cheese Whiz
Cool-Whip
Fresh or frozen ground beef

Cream cheese, it freezes well for
 storage
Refrigerated shredded Cheddar
 cheese, it freezes well
Pudding mixes, instant and cooked
 kind
Several kinds of pasta, dry not fresh
English muffins, they freeze well
 for later use
Taco seasoning mix
Chili powder
Dried onions, chopped
Dried minced garlic
Ground cinnamon
Ground nutmeg
Pecans
English walnuts
Bisquick baking mix
Parmesan cheese, dry grated
Self-rising flour
Dry noodles
Sugar, granulated
Brown sugar
Flour, regular white or whole wheat
Vanilla
Eggs
Peanut butter

The Cook's Notes

Table of Contents

Appetizers

&

Beverages

EASY PARTY RYE BREAD SNACKS

2 loaves party rye bread   1 lb. Italian sausage
  (the sm. size bread)   1 lb. Velveeta cheese
1 lb. ground beef

FRY ground beef and sausage together. Drain. Add a 1 pound
bar of Velveeta cheese. Stir until melted. Drop the mixture on
party rye bread. Bake 10 minutes at 350°. This can be frozen to
be used later.

GLAZED SAUSAGE BITES
(OR TINY HOT DOGS)

1 C. apple jelly   2 T. prepared horseradish
2 T. mustard   24 cocktail sausages or hot
                                              dogs (cocktail size)

Combine apple jelly, mustard and horseradish in skillet; mix well.
Bring to a boil. Add the sausages. SIMMER until sausages are
heated through and glazed. Serve hot.

SIMPLE SALSA APPETIZER

1-8 oz. pkg. cream cheese   Bag of tortilla chips
½ C. salsa (hot or med.)

Place cream cheese on serving plate. Top with salsa. Serve with
tortilla chips. You can make this a low fat recipe if you wish, just
use fat-free cream cheese and low-fat tortilla chips.

SAUSAGE CHEESE BALLS

2½ C. Bisquick   1 lb. cheese, grated
1 lb. pork sausage,   (Cheddar
  ground fine   or your favorite)

Mix all ingredients in large bowl. Shape into small balls and bake
at 350° for 15 to 20 minutes. Makes about 65 balls.
These are very good.

HAM AND CHEESE BALL

1-4½ oz. can deviled ham
8 oz. cream cheese, softened

8 oz. Cheddar cheese, shredded

Shape deviled ham into ball. Mold cream cheese around ham ball. Roll in Cheddar cheese. Chill, wrapped in plastic wrap, until serving time. Serve with assorted crackers.

FAVORITE AFTER-DINNER DRINK

1 C. bourbon
1 C. strong coffee, <u>COOLED</u>

1 qt. vanilla ice cream

Mix all ingredients in blender until smooth. Serve immediately in champagne glasses. Makes 4 to 6 servings.

PUNCH
(GOOD FOR ANY OCCASION)

1 lg. can Hawaiian punch
2 pkgs. cherry Kool-Aid
2 C. sugar

3 qts. water
1 lg. bottle 7-Up

Mix in large punch bowl the Hawaiian punch, Kool-Aid, sugar and water. Add the 7-Up just before serving. Add large pieces of ice. (Always use a large piece of ice in beverages, it takes longer to melt and doesn't dilute the beverage).

SHERBET PUNCH

2 lg. bottles 7-Up

½ gal. sherbet, use your favorite flavor, (I like lime or pineapple)

Pour the 7-Up into a large punch bowl, then add the entire ½ gallon of sherbet. Gently stir and mix with the 7-Up.
Very good for any occasion.

PINA COLADA COOLER

2 C. unsweetened pineapple juice, CHILLED
½ C. cream of coconut mixture, CHILLED (this can be purchased in the grocery store)

2 C. club soda, CHILLED
1 pt. vanilla ice cream

In large pitcher, mix the pineapple juice and cream of coconut. Stir in the club soda. Serve in glasses. Top with the ice cream. Makes 4-10 ounce servings.

SPARKLING CRANBERRY PUNCH

2 qts. cranberry cocktail, chilled
1-6 oz. can frozen pink lemonade concentrate, thawed

1 qt. sparkling water, chilled

In large punch bowl, combine cranberry cocktail and lemonade concentrate. Stir in sparkling water. Add large mold of ice. Serve immediately. To keep the punch from getting diluted, freeze a mold out of some cranberry juice.

BACON AND CHEDDAR RANCH DIP

Mix 1 ounce packet ranch party dip with 1 PINT sour cream. Add ¼ cup bacon bits and 1 cup shredded Cheddar cheese. Mix together and serve.

EASY SPINACH DIP

1-10 oz. box frozen chopped spinach
8 oz. chopped water chestnuts

1 pkg. dried cream of vegetable SOUP MIX
1 C. sour cream
1 C. mayonnaise

Thaw and drain spinach. Mix ingredients well, cover and refrigerate overnight. Serve in a hollowed out round loaf of rye bread. You can also serve this with potato chips.

EASY TACO DIP

8 oz. cream cheese
8 oz. sour cream
1 pkg. dry taco seasoning mix
12 oz. bottle hot or mild taco
  sauce (choose the one you
  like)

1 C. shredded lettuce
1 C. diced tomatoes
½ C. diced green olives
½ C. ripe olives, if desired

Mix well the sour cream, cream cheese and taco mix. Mound in the center of serving dish and pour over the taco sauce, then layer the chopped lettuce, diced tomatoes, green onions and ripe olives. Top all with the shredded taco cheese. Serve with tortilla chips.

DILL DIP

8 oz. sour cream
¾ C. Miracle Whip
1 tsp. dill weed

1 tsp. seasoned salt
1 tsp. onion juice

Mix all ingredients in small bowl and refrigerate. Serve with assorted crackers.

The greatest trials bring the greatest strength.

Breads

&

Breakfast

EASY MUFFINS

2 C. baking mix (I use Bisquick)   ⅔ C. COLD water or milk
3 T. sugar   ½ tsp. vanilla
1 egg

Heat oven to 400°. Grease 12 medium muffin cups or spray them with a non-stick baking spray.
Mix all the ingredients with a spoon; beat for ½ minute. Fill the muffin cups ⅔ full. Bake for 12 to 15 minutes. Makes 12 muffins.
VARIATION: Sprinkle the tops with a mixture of cinnamon and sugar <u>before</u> baking.

HERB BISCUITS

¼ C. margarine, melted   ½ tsp. dill seed
1½ tsp. minced parsley   1-10 count can refrigerator
3 T. Parmesan cheese   buttermilk biscuits

Combine margarine, parsley, cheese and dill seed in 9" baking pan. Cut biscuits into halves. Arrange biscuits in pan, turning to coat with butter mixture. Bake at 425° for 12 to 15 minutes. Yields 20 biscuits.

QUICK BREADSTICKS

12 hot dog buns   1 tsp. basil
1 C. butter, SOFTENED   ¼ tsp. garlic powder

Cut buns into quarters lengthwise. Blend butter, basil and garlic powder in small bowl. Spread on buns, place on baking sheet. Bake at 250° for 1½ hours until crisp. Cool and store in freezer for any leftover.
NOTE: This takes longer to fix these breadsticks, but they are quick and easy to warm up. Store them in freezer until ready to warm.

"For we walk by faith, not by sight."

PARMESAN BISCUITS

2-10 count cans refrigerator   1 C. Parmesan cheese
  biscuits
½ C. butter or margarine, melted

Dip each biscuit into melted butter or margarine; roll in Parmesan cheese to coat. Place on baking sheet. Bake at 425° until golden brown. Makes 20 servings.

QUICK BISCUITS

2 C. self-rising flour   1 C. heavy cream

In a large bowl, combine the flour and cream. Turn out onto a floured board; knead for 5 minutes or until no longer sticky. On a floured surface, roll dough to a ½" thickness. Cut into 3" biscuits. Place on a greased baking sheet. Bake at 450° for 8 to 10 minutes. NOTE: If you don't have self-rising flour, add 1 tablespoon baking powder and 1 teaspoon salt to 2 cups flour.

TOASTY BREAD SNACKS

½ C. soft margarine   1 Vienna bread loaf, sliced
⅓ C. CRUSHED French fried
  onions OR ⅓ C. grated
  Parmesan cheese

Combine margarine and onions; spread on 1 side of each bread slice. Place bread slices, spread-side up on ungreased cookie sheet. Bake at 400° for 12 to 15 minutes or until lightly browned. NOTE: These are good with a meal or to serve with your favorite beverage. Especially good with a glass of wine or beer.

BEER BUNS

3 C. buttermilk baking mix   1 C. beer
¼ C. sugar

Combine baking mix and sugar in bowl. Add beer; mix with fork until moistened. Spoon into greased muffin cups. Bake at 400° for 20 minutes or until golden brown. Makes 12 servings.

BLUEBERRY ICE CREAM MUFFINS

1 C. self-rising flour
1 C. vanilla ice cream, softened

1 C. blueberries, well-drained

Combine flour and ice cream in bowl; mix with fork until moistened. Fold in blueberries. Spoon into paper-lined muffin cups. Bake at 350° for 20 minutes or until golden brown. Makes 12 servings.

CRESCENT ALMOND ROLLS

¼ C. butter or margarine
1¼ C. SIFTED powdered sugar
1 T. flour

1 egg yolk
¼ C. finely GROUND almonds
2 cans (8 oz. each) refrigerated crescent rolls

Cream butter, sugar and flour. Beat in egg yolk; add almonds. Spread each triangle of dough with almond mixture. Roll up and bake according to package directions for crescent rolls.
NOTE: One can (8 ounces) of almond paste may be used in place of the homemade mixture.

CINNAMON STICKS

1 C. butter or margarine, melted
1½ C. sugar

2 T. cinnamon
1 loaf UNSLICED white bread

Melt butter in large shallow skillet. Mix sugar and cinnamon in medium bowl. Remove crusts from bread and cut into approximately 1x1x2" sticks. Roll bread sticks quickly in butter (to just coat the bread surface), then in cinnamon sugar. Place on cookie sheet. Bake at 425° for 12 minutes. Cool on rack. Wrap in foil to store. May be frozen. If you do freeze them, warm in foil in regular oven before serving.

PRALINE CRACKERS

Spread 27 whole graham crackers (broken in ½) in a single layer in a jelly roll pan. Heat 2 sticks of margarine and 1 cup of brown sugar to boiling point and continue boiling for 2 minutes, stirring constantly. Add 1 cup of FINELY chopped nuts and pour the mixture over the crackers, covering them as completely as possible. Bake at 350° for 10 minutes. Separate crackers while still warm and cool on wire rack. Makes 4 dozen.

ENGLISH EGG MUFFIN

2 T. chopped green pepper
2 T. margarine or butter
6 eggs, beaten
⅓ C .milk

Salt and pepper to taste
3 English muffins, SPLIT and
  TOASTED
6 slices Velveeta cheese

Sauté peppers in margarine; add combined eggs, milk and seasonings. Cook slowly, stirring occasionally, until eggs are set. For each sandwich, top muffin ½ with egg and cheese. BROIL UNTIL CHEESE BEGINS TO MELT. WATCH VERY CAREFULLY SO THE CHEESE DOES NOT BURN. Makes 6 sandwiches.

BISCUIT MONKEY BREAD

4-10 count cans refrigerator
  biscuits
1¾ C. sugar

1 tsp. cinnamon
½ C. finely chopped pecans
1 C. margarine or butter,
  melted

Cut biscuits into quarters. Roll in mixture of sugar and cinnamon. Mix pecans with ¾ of the margarine. Alternate layers of biscuits and pecan mixture in greased tube pan. Bring remaining cinnamon mixture and margarine to a boil in saucepan. Pour over the biscuits. Bake at 350° for 25 minutes. Makes 16 servings.

*We may give without loving, but we cannot
love without giving.*

PINEAPPLE COFFEE CAKE

2 C. baking mix (I use Bisquick)
3 T. sugar
1 egg
⅔ C. cold water or milk

TOPPING MIX:
2 T. margarine, melted
¼ C. brown sugar
1-8¾ oz. can crushed
   pineapple, DRAINED

Mix all the ingredients together with spoon until smooth. Pour into 9" pan that has been sprayed with non-stick baking spray. Pour the melted margarine over the batter. Sprinkle the brown sugar over the top. Spoon the drained pineapple over the sugar; gently spread evenly. Bake for 20 to 25 minutes or until lightly browned. Cut into squares. Makes 8 servings.

APPLE PANCAKES

2 C. Bisquick
1 egg
1⅓ C. milk

2 C. finely chopped apple (I
   like yellow delicious)
2 T. sugar

Beat all ingredients with rotary beater until smooth. Fold in the apples. Fry or grill as usual, turning when bubbles appear. Serve hot with your favorite syrup.

SEVEN-UP PANCAKES

1 egg, well beaten
1 T. melted shortening

10 T. 7-Up
1 C. buttermilk pancake mix

Combine egg and shortening in bowl. Stir in 6 tablespoons 7-Up. Add the pancake mix; blend well. Stir in remaining 7-Up. Spoon onto hot greased griddle. Bake until brown on both sides. Serve with your favorite syrup.

The only wise speed at which to live is......
God's speed.

OVEN-BAKED FRENCH TOAST

1 loaf French bread	¼ C. honey
4 lg. eggs	½ tsp. nutmeg
½ C. half and half	½ tsp. vanilla

PREHEAT oven to 500°. GREASE 2 large baking sheets or spray them with non-stick vegetables spray.

Cut the French loaf crosswise into 1" diagonal slices. In a 13x9" baking dish. place the bread slices. In a medium bowl, whisk the eggs, half and half, honey, nutmeg and vanilla. Pour the egg mixture over the bread and turn the slices to coat evenly. Let the bread soak until the egg mixture is absorbed, about 15 minutes. Place the bread on the prepared baking sheets. Bake until golden, 8 to 10 minutes on each side. Transfer to serving dishes. Top each serving with strawberries or syrup.

APPLE BREAKFAST PIE

1 ready-to-use graham cracker crust	⅓ C. sugar
	¼ tsp. vanilla
1 pkg. cream cheese, softened	1-19 to 21 oz. can apple pie filling
1 egg yolk	1 tsp. cinnamon
1 egg	1 C. granola

Beat the egg yolk and brush on crust. Bake in a preheated 375° oven for 5 minutes. Set aside. Reduce the oven to 350°. In a small mixing bowl, beat the cream cheese until smooth. Add egg, sugar and vanilla. Mix well. Spoon into prepared crust. Top with the pie filling; bake for 15 minutes. Sprinkle with granola and continue to bake 10 minutes or more until granola is toasted. Cool to room temperature and serve. This pie can be chilled and then reheated to serve.

Children are a great comfort in your old age,
and they help you reach it faster, too!

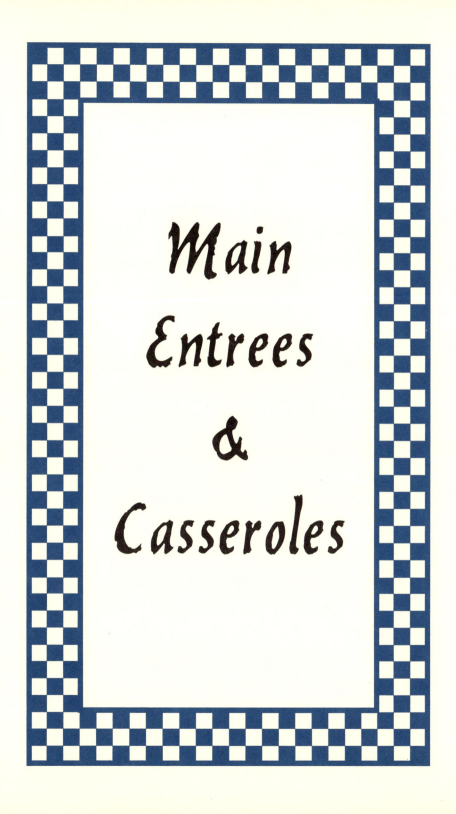

Main

Entrees

&

Casseroles

YUMMY APRICOT CHICKEN

4 chicken breast halves with
skin removed

2-4 oz. jars baby food
apricots
4 T. Dijon mustard

Place chicken in baking pan. Mix and spoon over chicken. Bake covered 40 minutes at 350°. Baste with the drippings and bake for 10 minutes UNCOVERED.
NOTE: Be prepared to serve seconds.

EASY CHICKEN AND NOODLES

1 can cream of chicken soup
½ C. milk
⅓ C. grated Parmesan cheese
⅛ tsp. pepper

3 C. cooked med. noodles
(cook 3 C. dry noodles)
2 C. cubed, cooked chicken
(you can use canned)

In saucepan, combine soup, milk, cheese and pepper; add cooked noodles and chicken. Over low heat, heat through. Stir often.

SUPER CHICKEN CASSEROLE

4 C. chopped, cooked
chicken (you can use canned
white chicken)
1 can cream of chicken soup
8 oz. sour cream

1-8 oz. pkg. corn bread
STUFFING MIX
2 C. chicken broth

Place chicken in large baking dish that has been sprayed with non-stick spray. Mix soup and cream in bowl. Pour over the chicken. Combine stuffing mix and chicken broth in bowl. Spread over the chicken in the baking dish. Bake for 45 minutes or until brown.

Just about the time you think you can make both ends meet, somebody moves the ends.

11

SHIRLEY'S BAKED CHICKEN

2 C. chopped, cooked
  chicken (you can use
  canned chicken)
2 C. chopped celery
⅓ C. chopped pecans, opt.
2 T. minced onion

¾ C. mayonnaise
2 T. lemon juice
1½ C. shredded Cheddar
  cheese
1 C. potato chips

Spray 2-quart baking dish with non-stick cooking spray. Combine chicken, celery, nuts, onion, mayonnaise and lemon juice. Place mixture in 2-quart casserole. Sprinkle with cheese and potato chips. Bake at 350° for 25 to 30 minutes.

SCRAMBLED EGGS AND CHICKEN

1 can condensed cream of
  chicken soup
8 eggs, beaten

Dash of pepper
2 T. margarine or butter
Chopped fresh parsley

TOPPING: 5 slices American cheese

In medium bowl, stir soup until smooth. Gradually blend in eggs and pepper. In 10" skillet over low heat, melt margarine. Pour in egg mixture. As eggs begin to set, stir lightly so uncooked egg flows to bottom. Cook until SET but still moist. Top with American cheese slices until cheese melts. Remove from heat at once and serve.

CHICKEN POCKETS

2 C. cooked chicken, diced
3 T. melted butter or chicken
3 oz. cream cheese, softened
¼ tsp. salt

Dash of pepper
1 T. chopped onion
8 oz. can refrigerated
  crescent rolls
½ C. seasoned bread
  crumbs

Blend cream cheese with 2 tablespoons melted butter. Add salt, pepper, onion and chicken, mixing well. Separate the crescent dough into 4 rectangles, pressing perforations to seal. Spoon ½ cup of chicken mixture into the center of each rectangle. Bring the 4 corners together, twisting to seal. Brush the tops with remaining melted butter and sprinkle with bread crumbs. Bake on ungreased baking sheet for 20 minutes at 350°. Serves 4.

CHINESE CHICKEN

2 C. sliced celery
½ lb. boneless, skinless chicken
breast meat, cut into bite size
pieces
1-10 oz. can cream of
mushroom soup
½ can water

1-14 oz. can chop suey
vegetables, drained and
rinsed
½ tsp. salt
½ tsp. pepper

Sauté celery in large, sprayed non-stick skillet for 2 minutes. Add the chicken pieces and sauté for 2 minutes more. Add the remaining ingredients. Mix well. Simmer, uncovered, for 25 minutes. Add more water if it is too dry. Serve over cooked white rice (not the MINUTE).

PARMESAN CHICKEN

½ C. grated Parmesan cheese
¼ C. dry bread crumbs
1 tsp. dried oregano
1 tsp. dried parsley flakes
¼ tsp. paprika

¼ tsp. salt
¼ tsp. pepper
6 boneless, skinless chicken
breast halves
¼ C. butter or margarine,
melted

In a large bowl, combine the first 7 ingredients. Dip chicken in butter and then into crumb mixture. Place in a greased 15x10x1" baking pan. Bake, uncovered, at 400° for 20 to 25 minutes or until chicken is tender and juices run clear.

QUICK CHICKEN OR TURKEY CASSEROLE

3 C. cubed, cooked chicken or
turkey (you can use canned)
2-10¾ oz. cans condensed
cream of chicken or celery
soup
1-16 oz. pkg. frozen mixed
vegetables

1 tsp. poultry seasoning
½ tsp. garlic salt
2 C. biscuit mix
1½ C. milk
1 tsp. parsley flakes

Heat oven to 450°. Mix chicken, soup, vegetables, poultry seasoning and garlic salt into 13x9x2" baking dish that has been lightly sprayed with non-stick spray. Stir baking mix and milk until blended. Spread over chicken mixture. Sprinkle with parsley. Bake 30 to 35 minutes or until light golden brown.

FAVORITE CHICKEN POTPIE

⅓ C. margarine, melted
⅓ C. flour
1¾ C. chicken broth, canned
⅔ C. milk

2 C. chopped, cooked chicken(use canned if you don't want to cook it)
Salt and pepper to taste
1-10 oz. pkg. frozen mixed vegetables, thawed
1 pkg. prepared pie crust (the 1 that has 2 crusts in it)

Blend margarine, flour, salt and pepper in the saucepan. Cook over medium heat for 1 minute, stirring constantly. Stir in chicken broth and milk. Cook until thickened, stirring constantly. Stir in the chicken and vegetables. Spoon into a 2-quart pastry-lined crust. Top with remaining crust. Seal the edges; cut the vents in top. Bake at 350° for 30 minutes or until golden brown.

EASY CHICKEN AND PASTA

2 C. cooked chicken, CUBED
1-10¾ oz. can cream of chicken soup

1 pkg. frozen seasoned pasta and vegetable combination
½ C. water

In a skillet, heat 1 tablespoon oil. Add the chicken and cook until browned. Add soup, ½ cup water and pasta and vegetable combination. Cover and cook for 5 minutes or until vegetables are tender, stirring often. Use low heat!

OVEN FRIED MUSTARD CHICKEN

⅓ C. bread crumbs
⅓ C. flour
¼ tsp. paprika
⅓ C. Dijon mustard

Salt and pepper
1 T. butter or margarine
4 boneless chicken breast halves (about 1½ lbs.)

Heat the oven to 425°. Combine the bread crumbs, flour and paprika. Combine the mustard, ¾ teaspoon salt, ¼ teaspoon pepper and 2 tablespoons water. Melt the butter. Line a shallow pan with foil and spray with non-stick cooking spray. Dip the chicken breasts in the mustard mixture, then coat them with the crumb mixture. Put in the prepared pan. Drizzle the butter over the chicken. Bake until browned and cooked through, 10 to 15 minutes, or until tender and not pink.

ZESTY CHICKEN ITALIAN

6 pcs. chicken breasts
1½ C. spaghetti sauce

6 slices sliced mozzarella
 cheese
Parmesan cheese

In a non-stick skillet, heat 1 tablespoon oil. Sauté the chicken until tender. Take the chicken out and drain on paper towels. Wipe the skillet clean with a paper towel. Put the chicken back into the skillet. SPOON THE SPAGHETTI SAUCE OVER THE CHICKEN BREASTS. TOP EACH PIECE OF CHICKEN WITH A SLICE OF CHEESE. SPRINKLE WITH PARMESAN CHEESE. Cook over a very low heat until sauce is heated and the cheese is melted.

CHICKEN STUFFING CASSEROLE

1-10¾ oz. can condensed
 cream of mushroom soup
1 C. milk
1-7 oz. pkg. herb seasoned
 stuffing mix

2 C. cubed, cooked chicken
2 C. cooked broccoli
 flowerets
2 stalks celery, finely
 chopped
1½ C. shredded Swiss
 cheese
 (6 oz.), divided

Heat oven to 375°. Meanwhile, in large bowl, stir soup until smooth. Gradually stir in milk. Add the stuffing mix, chicken, broccoli, celery and 1 cup of the cheese. Spread mixture in greased 2-quart oblong baking dish. Bake for 20 minutes. Top with REMAINING CHEESE; bake until cheese melts.

CHICKEN BROCCOLI CASSEROLE
(MICROWAVE)

2 med. boneless chicken
 breasts, cut up to bite size
1 pkg. frozen chopped
 broccoli, thawed

2 C. shredded cheese
1 can cream of chicken soup
 (or cream of celery)

Mix all ingredients in microwave dish. Cover. Microwave on HIGH for 25 minutes. Stir several times during cooking time. Let stand in microwave for 5 minutes. Serve.

CHICKEN BISCUIT CUPS

2-10 oz. tubes refrigerated
 biscuits
2 C. (8 oz.) shredded Cheddar
 cheese, divided
1⅓ C. crisp rice cereal
 (Rice Krispies

1 C. cubed <u>COOKED</u> chicken
1-10¾ oz. condensed cream
 of mushroom soup,
 undiluted
1-10 oz. pkg. frozen chopped
 broccoli, cooked and
 drained

Place biscuits in greased muffin cups, pressing dough over the bottom and up the sides. Add 1 tablespoon cheese and cereal to each cup. Combine chicken, soup and broccoli; spoon into cups. Bake at 375° for 20 to 25 minutes or until bubbly. Sprinkle with remaining cheese. Makes 8 to 10 servings.

QUICK AND EASY CHICKEN CORDON BLEU

4 chicken cutlets (you can used
 turkey if you like), CUBED
½ tsp. dried oregano leaves,
 crushed
1 T. vegetable oil

1 T. margarine
Dash pepper
4 ham slices, thin sliced
4 provolone cheese slices

SPRINKLE THE CHICKEN OR TURKEY with oregano. Heat oil and margarine in large skillet. Add the chicken or turkey, COOK 8 minutes or until no longer pink in the center, turning after 4 minutes. Season with pepper. TOP EACH CUTLET WITH HAM AND CHEESE. COVER. CONTINUE COOKING 3 TO 5 MINUTES OR UNTIL CHEESE HAS JUST MELTED.

CHICKEN ITALIANO

½ C. grated Parmesan cheese
2 T. minced parsley
1 tsp. dried oregano
1 clove garlic, minced

½ tsp. black pepper
2 whole chicken breasts,
 boned and skinned
3 T. butter, melted

Combine cheese, parsley, oregano, garlic and pepper. Dip chicken in melted butter, then in cheese mixture. Place in shallow baking dish. Drizzle the remaining butter over the chicken. Bake at 375° for 25 minutes or until tender.

ESCALLOPED CHICKEN

5 slices white bread, cut into
cubes (I like stale bread best)
½ C. chopped celery
3 eggs, beaten
1-10¾ oz. can cream of
mushroom soup

1 C. sliced mushrooms (I use
canned)
1 sm. onion, chopped
2 C. diced, cooked chicken
(you can use white canned
chicken)
2 C. shredded Cheddar
cheese
1¾ C. mayonnaise

Mix all the ingredients together. Spread in well-greased 2-quart
casserole at 350° for 45 minutes. Serve at once.

TURKEY OR CHICKEN SUPER SUPPER

2-10 oz. pkgs. frozen broccoli,
thawed
10 slices cooked turkey or
chicken
2 cans cream of chicken soup

¾ C. mayonnaise
1 T. lemon juice
1 C. shredded Cheddar
cheese

Spray baking dish with non-stick cooking spray. Layer broccoli
and turkey in 9x13" baking dish. Mix soup, mayonnaise and lemon
juice in bowl. Pour over turkey and broccoli. Top with cheese.
Bake at 350° for 40 minutes.

EASY CHICKEN AND VEGETABLE
STIR-FRY

2 chicken breasts, boneless
and skinless, cut into
sm. strips

⅓ C. (2.8 oz. can)
French fried onions
21 oz. pkg. teriyaki stir-fry,
frozen vegetable
combination. Get the one
that has the sauce package
included.

Heat 1 tablespoon oil in non-stick skillet; stir-fry the chicken until
browned; about 5 minutes. Add the vegetables, stir-fry until crisp-
tender. Stir in contents of sauce package and cook until hot.
Microwave the French fried onions for 1 minute. Sprinkle the onions
over the stir-fry mixture. Serve over hot, cooked rice.

QUICK CHICKEN AND BROCCOLI PIE

1-10 oz. pkg. frozen chopped broccoli
3 C. shredded Cheddar cheese (12 oz.) or use your favorite cheese
1½ C. cut-up COOKED chicken (you can use canned chicken)

⅔ C. chopped onion
1⅓ C. milk
3 eggs
¼ C. baking mix (I use Bisquick)
¼ tsp. salt
¼ tsp. pepper

Heat oven to 400°. Grease pie plate (10"). Rinse broccoli under running cold water to thaw; drain thoroughly. Mix broccoli, 2 cups of the cheese, the chicken and onion in plate. Beat milk, eggs, baking mix, salt and pepper until smooth; 15 seconds in blender on high or 1 minute with hand beater. Pour into plate. Bake until knife inserted in center comes out clean. This is usually 25 to 30 minutes. Top with the remaining cheese. Bake 1 or 2 minutes longer, just until cheese melts. Cool 5 minutes.
NOTE: This pie forms its own crust so you do not need a pie pastry shell.

GOOD AND EASY TACO PIE

1¼ lbs. ground chuck
1 pkg. taco seasoning mix
½ C. water
½ C. chunky salsa
1-8 oz. can crescent dinner rolls (the refrigerated ones)

1½ C. crushed corn chips
1-8 oz. carton sour cream
6 slices American cheese
Shredded lettuce
Sliced black olives
Diced tomatoes

Brown meat in large skillet; drain. Add the seasoning mix, water and salsa; simmer for 5 minutes. Spread the crescent roll dough in 10" pie plate to form crust press edges together at the seams. Sprinkle 1 cup corn chips on crust bottom, reserving remaining ½ cup. Spoon on meat mixture. Spread sour cream over meat. Cover with cheese slices; sprinkle on remaining ½ cup of crushed corn chips. Bake at 375° for 20 minutes or until crust is golden brown. Serve with lettuce, olives and tomatoes. Kids love this!!!

QUICK AND EASY BEEF HASH

1 lb. lean ground chuck	¼ tsp. pepper
1 sm. onion, chopped	1 C. salsa
3 C. frozen potatoes O'Brien	Green onion and ripe olive
½ tsp. salt	slices, opt.

Brown ground chuck and onion in large skillet over medium heat 8 to 10 minutes or until no longer pink. Pour off drippings. Stir in potatoes, salt and pepper. Increase heat to medium-high and cook for 5 minutes, stirring occasionally. Stir in salsa. Continue cooking 8 to 10 minutes or until potatoes are lightly browned, stirring occasionally. Garnish with green onion and ripe olive slices, if desired.

CRUNCHY ONION BURGERS

1½ lb. ground beef or chuck	¾ tsp. salt
1⅓ C. (2.8 oz. can) French fried onions	¼ tsp. pepper
	6 hamburger buns

Mix the beef and ⅔ cup French fried onions and salt and pepper. Shape into 6 burgers. Grill or fry for 10 minutes or until no longer pink in center, turning once. Serve on buns and top with more of the canned French fried onions, if desired.

BEEF CHILI MACARONI

1 lb. beef cubed steaks, chopped as directed below	1½ C. uncooked wagon wheel pasta
2-14½ oz. cans chili seasoned chunky tomatoes	1 med. onion, chopped
	¾ C. shredded Monterey Jack or Cheddar cheese

Cut beef steaks lengthwise into 1" wide strips, then crosswise into 1" pieces. Spray Dutch oven with vegetable cooking spray, heat over medium-high heat until hot. Add the beef and onion to pan; cook and stir for 3 minutes. Stir in tomatoes, pasta and ½ cup water into pan. Bring to a boil; reduce heat to low. Cover tightly; simmer 20 minutes or until pasta is tender. Sprinkle with cheese before serving. Makes 4 servings.

SHIRLEY'S WHITE CASTLES

1 lb. ground chuck
⅓ C. finely chopped onions

1 egg, beaten
Salt and pepper to taste

Mix all the ingredients together until well mixed. Spread a <u>thin</u> layer on each side of small bun. Melt 2 tablespoons of butter and margarine in large skillet; use medium heat, DO NOT BURN! Place each bun in skillet with meat side down. Cook slowly, COVERED, until meat is done (just a few minutes). Remove from skillet and put the 2 halves together. Serve at once!

CHEESEBURGER MACARONI

1 C. elbow macaroni,
  UNCOOKED
1 lb. ground chuck
1 med. onion, chopped (or
  equivalent in dried onions)

1-14½ oz. can stewed
  tomatoes (you can use the
  Italian canned tomatoes
  if you like)
¼ C. tomato catsup
1 C. (4 oz.) shredded
  Cheddar cheese

Cook the pasta according to package directions. Drain well. (Do not overcook). In large skillet, brown the meat with onions; drain. Season with salt and pepper. Stir in tomatoes, catsup and pasta, heat through. Top with the cheese.
This is a recipe that kids really like.

QUICK VEGETABLES AND BEEF

1 T. vegetable oil
1 C. broccoli flowerets (fresh
  or frozen)

1-19 oz. can <u>chunky</u>
  vegetable beef soup
2 T. Worcestershire sauce
2 C. <u>COOKED</u> RICE

In saucepan, over medium heat, heat the oil. Add the broccoli and cook until tender-crisp. Add the soup, Worcestershire sauce and rice. Heat through.

EASY SPAGHETTI PIE

1 lb. ground beef	⅓ C. grated Parmesan
½ C. chopped onion	cheese
¼ C. chopped green pepper	¾ C. shredded mozzarella
1-15½ oz. jar spaghetti sauce	cheese
8 oz. spaghetti, HOT, COOKED	2 eggs, beaten
AND DRAINED	2 tsp. butter
1½ C. cottage cheese	

Cook ground beef, onion and green pepper, stirring to separate meat. Drain off fat. Stir in spaghetti sauce; mix well. Combine spaghetti, Parmesan cheese, eggs and butter in large bowl; mix well. Place this in the bottom of 13x9" pan that has been sprayed with non-stick spray. Spread the cottage cheese over the top. Pour the sauce mixture over the cottage cheese. Sprinkle mozzarella cheese over top. Bake in preheated oven at 350° for about 20 minutes.

SLOPPY JOES

1 lb. ground beef (I use	1 T. sugar
ground chuck)	2 T. mustard
1 C. green peppers, chopped	1 T. vinegar
1 C. onions, chopped	1 C. catsup

BROWN ground beef, then add the other ingredients. SIMMER for 15 minutes. Serve on buns of your choice.

HAMBURGER SPREAD SANDWICHES

1-10¼ oz. can condensed	1¼ tsp. salt
tomato soup	¼ tsp. pepper
½ C. shredded American	1 lb. ground beef
cheese	8 hamburger buns, sliced
¼ C. brown sugar	in ½
1 T. finely chopped onion	

Mix together all ingredients. TOAST the split bun halves. Spread bun halves with the meat mixture, sealing to edges. Broil 6" away from heat for about 8 minutes, watching carefully. Serve these open face, 2 halves per serving.

EASY CHEESEBURGER PIE

1 lb. ground chuck
¾ C. chopped onion
½ tsp. salt
¼ tsp. pepper
1½ C. milk

¾ C. baking mix (like
 Bisquick)
3 eggs
2 tomatoes
 1½ C. shredded Cheddar or
 American cheese

Heat oven to 400°. Grease pie plate (use a 10" pie plate). Brown beef and onion; drain. Stir in salt and pepper. Spread in plate. Beat milk, baking mix and eggs until smooth, use mixer or blender. Pour into plate. Bake for 25 minutes. Top with tomatoes; sprinkle with the cheese. Bake until a knife inserted in center comes out clean, 5 to 8 minutes. Cool for 5 minutes. Makes 6 to 8 servings.

QUICK AND EASY LASAGNE PIE

½ C. creamed sm. curd
  cottage cheese
1 lb. ground chuck
1½ C. shredded mozzarella
  cheese (will use separately)

½ tsp. salt
½ tsp. dried oregano
1-6 oz. can tomato paste

Spread cottage cheese in greased 9" pie plate. Cook ground chuck, drain. Stir in ½ cup mozzarella cheese, salt, oregano and tomato paste; spoon over cottage cheese.

½ C. milk
2 eggs

½ C. baking mix (I use
 Bisquick)

Stir milk, eggs and baking mix with fork until blended. Pour in plate. Bake for 30 to 35 minutes or until knife inserted in the center comes out clean. Sprinkle with the remaining cheese. Bake for 1 or 2 minutes more until cheese is melted.

*Praise to a child is as water
to a thirsty plant.*

BEST CROCK POT CHILI

2 lbs. lean ground chuck
1 lg. onion, chopped
1 clove garlic, minced (you
   can use dried minced garlic)

3 cans tomato soup
3-16 oz. cans kidney beans
1 T. chili powder

Brown ground beef with onion and garlic in skillet, stirring until ground beef is crumbly; DRAIN. Place in 3½-quart CROCK POT. Add soup, beans and chili powder; mix well. Cook on LOW for 6 to 8 hours, stirring occasionally. Makes 8 servings.

BEEF OVEN PORCUPINES

1 lb. ground chuck
½ C. rice
1 C. chopped onion
Celery salt, garlic powder, salt
   and pepper to taste

1-15 oz. can tomato sauce
2 tsp. Worcestershire sauce
1 C. water

Combine ground chuck, rice, onion and seasonings in bowl; mix well. Shape into small balls. Place in 8" baking dish that has been sprayed with non-stick baking spray. Mix tomato sauce, Worcestershire sauce and water in bowl. Pour over meatballs. Bake, COVERED, at 350° for 45 minutes or until done and no longer pink in center.
NOTE: This is a good recipe to fix in your crock pot. Allow 4 to 6 hours if you use a crock pot.

MICROWAVE SWEET AND SOUR MEATBALLS

1 lb. ground chuck
1 onion, finely chopped
½ C. DRAINED, crushed
   pineapple
Salt to taste

1 can tomato soup
¼ C. packed brown sugar
3 T. lemon juice

Combine ground beef, onion, pineapple and salt in bowl; mix well. Shape into small balls. Combine soup, brown sugar and lemon juice in 8x8" glass dish that has been sprayed with non-stick baking spray. Microwave on HIGH for 7 minutes, stirring once. Add the meatballs. Microwave on MEDIUM for 5 minutes. Spoon sauce over sauce over meatballs; rotate dish. Microwave for 5 minutes longer. Serve over rice. Makes 6 servings.

TUNABURGERS

1-7 oz. can tuna, drained (I use
 tuna packed in water)
1 C. chopped celery
½ C. shredded mozzarella
 cheese
1 sm. onion, minced

¼ C. mayonnaise
¼ C. butter, softened
4 slices bread (use your
 favorite)

Combine the first 5 ingredients in bowl; mix well. Butter bread slices in 1 side. Spread the UNBUTTERED side of bread with the tuna mixture. Place on baking sheet, buttered side down. Bake at 350° for 15 minutes.

BEST-EVER TUNA CASSEROLE

1-10¾ oz. can condensed
 cream of celery soup
 drained
¼ C. milk
2 eggs, hard cooked, sliced

1 C. cooked peas
1 can tuna (about 7 oz.),
 and flaked (I use tuna
 packed in WATER)
½ C. slightly crushed potato
 chips

In 1-quart casserole, blend the soup and milk; stir in the DRAINED tuna, eggs and peas. Lightly toss together. Bake at 350° for 25 minutes or until hot; stir. TOP WITH THE CHIPS AND BAKE FOR 5 minutes more. Makes about 4 cups.

DELICIOUS EASY FLOUNDER AU GRATIN

¼ C. fine dry bread crumbs
¼ C. grated Parmesan
 cheese

1 lb. flounder (or if you
 prefer, you can use sole)
¼ C. mayonnaise

In shallow dish or on sheet of waxed paper, combine crumbs and cheese. Brush all sides of filets with real mayonnaise;then coat with the crumb mixture. Arrange in single layer in shallow baking pan. Bake at 375° for 20 to 25 minutes or until golden brown and fish flakes easily. Makes 4 servings.

BEER BATTER FISH

1 lb. fish ,your favorite (I like sole or perch)
3 to 4 T. Bisquick baking mix
1 C. Bisquick baking mix (keep this separate)

½ tsp. salt
1 egg
½ C. beer (your favorite)
Vegetable oil (to cover lg. heavy saucepan about 1½")

Heat vegetable oil in SAUCEPAN or deep fat fryer to 350°. Cut the fish into serving pieces. Lightly coat fish with the 3 or 4 tablespoons baking mix. Then mix the 1 cup of baking mix, the salt, egg and beer until smooth. Dip the fish into batter, letting the excess drip into bowl. Fry until golden brown, about 2 minutes or until golden brown. DRAIN ON PAPER TOWELS TO REMOVE EXCESS GREASE.

FISH FILETS ITALIAN

1 lb. fish filets (I use sole or
½ C. Italian salad dressing
2 T. lemon juice

½ tsp. pepper
½ tsp. paprika

Place fish in a baking dish that has been sprayed with non-stick cooking spray. Combine remaining ingredients and pour over fish. Bake at 375° for 10 to 20 minutes (or until fish flakes easily when tested with a fork).

PARMESAN FISH

¼ C. plain yogurt
1 T. lemon juice
1 tsp. Dijon mustard

1 lb. fish filets (I use sole or haddock)
½ C. grated Parmesan, divided

Mix yogurt, lemon juice and mustard in a small bowl. Place fish in a sprayed non-stick baking dish. Spread top side of fish with yogurt mixture. Sprinkle with most of the Parmesan, reserving some for serving. Bake uncovered at 400°. Bake for 10 to 15 minutes (or until fish flakes easily when tested with a fork). SPRINKLE WITH THE REMAINING PARMESAN CHEESE TO SERVE.

EASY FISH IN FOIL

1-16 oz. pkg. frozen, skinless
  cod, sole or perch filets
¼ C. margarine or butter,
  melted

1 tsp. salt
⅛ tsp. pepper

Heat oven to 450°. Remove frozen fish filets from package; wrap fish securely in 20x12" pieces of <u>heavy</u>-duty aluminum foil. Bake on ungreased cookie sheet for 25 minutes. Turn back foil; pour margarine over fish. Sprinkle with salt and pepper. Bake uncovered until fish flakes very easily with fork, about 10 minutes longer.

*Real love is helping someone who can't
return the favor.*

Soups

&

Salads

CREAM OF BROCCOLI SOUP

3½ C. milk (you will use
  separate)
1-10 oz. pkg. frozen broccoli,
  partially thawed

1 env. dried chicken noodle
  soup mix with diced chicken
  meat
1 T. flour

In medium saucepan, bring the 3 cups milk and broccoli to the boiling point, then simmer, stirring occasionally 5 minutes. Stir in chicken noodle soup mix. Blend the remaining milk and flour together and mix into the soup mixture. Bring just to the boiling point, then simmer, stirring several times, for 10 minutes or just until soup is slightly thickened and the broccoli is tender, not mushy. Very good.

QUICK AND YUMMY CORN CHOWDER

2-16 oz. cans cream style corn
1-10¾ oz. can cream of
  potato soup
1-13 oz. can evaporated milk
2 C. milk
¼ C. chopped green pepper

1 med. onion, chopped
  or 1 T. instant onion
1 tsp. salt
¼ tsp. pepper

Heat first 4 ingredients in large pot. While heating, sauté green peppers and onion; add to the corn mixture. Add the seasonings and serve hot. Serves 8.

QUICK VEGETABLE SOUP

You can make in 45 minutes.

2-12 oz. cans vegetable juice
  cocktail (V-8)
2 T. instant beef bouillon
1 sm. head cabbage,
  chopped fine
1 med. onion, chopped (you
  can use dry onion flakes)

3 sm. carrots, sliced thin (you
  can use canned carrots)
½ C. chopped celery
2 C. water

Combine all ingredients in large saucepan. Simmer, covered for about 45 minutes or until vegetables are tender.

CROCK POT CHILI SOUP

2 lbs. lean ground beef
1 lg. onion, chopped (I use
 dry onion flakes)
1 clove garlic, minced
 (I use dry)

3 cans tomato soup
3-16 oz. cans kidney beans
1 T. chili powder

Brown ground beef with onion and garlic in skillet, stirring until ground beef is crumbly. Drain. Place in 3½-quart crock pot. Add soup, beans and chili powder; mix well. Cook on LOW for 6 to 8 hours, (While you are at work or while you are sleeping).

HAM AND POTATO SOUP

1 T. margarine or butter
1 C. shredded cabbage
¼ lb. fully COOKED ham, cut
 into cubes (this is about
 1 C.)

1 can condensed cream of
 potato soup
1 soup can water
1 T. chopped fresh parsley, if
 desired

Melt margarine over medium heat in a 2-quart saucepan. Cook the cabbage and ham 5 minutes or just until cabbage is TENDER, stirring occasionally. Stir in remaining ingredients. Heat to boiling; REDUCE heat to low and heat through.

EASY FRENCH ONION SOUP

2 T. butter or margarine
1 lg. onion, sliced
1 tsp. sugar

1-10½ oz. can beef bouillon
1¼ C. water
2 T. Worcestershire sauce

Melt butter in medium size saucepan. Add the onion and sugar. Cook and stir for 5 to 10 minutes until lightly browned. Add bouillon, water and Worcestershire sauce; simmer for 10 to 15 minutes.

*Those who dine on the devils diet
soon become sickly saints.*

QUICK MACARONI SALAD

½ C. mayonnaise
1 tsp. prepared mustard
¼ tsp. salt
⅛ tsp. pepper

1 C. elbow macaroni (4 oz.),
  COOKED and drained
½ lb. hot dogs, sliced
¼ C. cubed American
  cheese
¼ C. sliced green onions,
  opt.

In large bowl, stir together first 4 ingredients. Add remaining ingredients; toss to coat well. Cover; chill at least 2 hours.

CHICKEN SALAD

¾ C. mayonnaise
3 T. Grey Poupon Dijon mustard
2 C. cooked chicken, cubed
  (you can use canned
  white chicken)

2 T. EACH: chopped
  pimento, pickle relish
  (omit pimento if desired)
½ C. slivered toasted
  almonds
2 eggs, hard cooked
1 T. onion, minced

Combine the mayonnaise and mustard. Toss dressing lightly with remaining ingredients. Chill. If desired, serve on a bed of lettuce. Serves 4.

QUICK BLUE CHEESE DRESSING

⅓ C. mayonnaise
⅓ C. crumbled blue cheese

1 C. plain yogurt

In small bowl, mix mayonnaise and blue cheese. Fold in yogurt. Cover and chill until serving time. Makes about 1½ cups.

Be a Christian, it's good for your health,
now and especially later.

QUICK FRENCH DRESSING

½ C. tomato catsup
½ C. salad oil
¼ C. apple cider vinegar
2 tsp. powdered sugar

1 clove garlic, split
¼ tsp. salt
Dash pepper

Combine ingredients in jar. Cover; shake vigorously. Chill to blend flavors. REMOVE the garlic, shake again before serving. Makes about 1½ cups.

The road to success is always under construction.

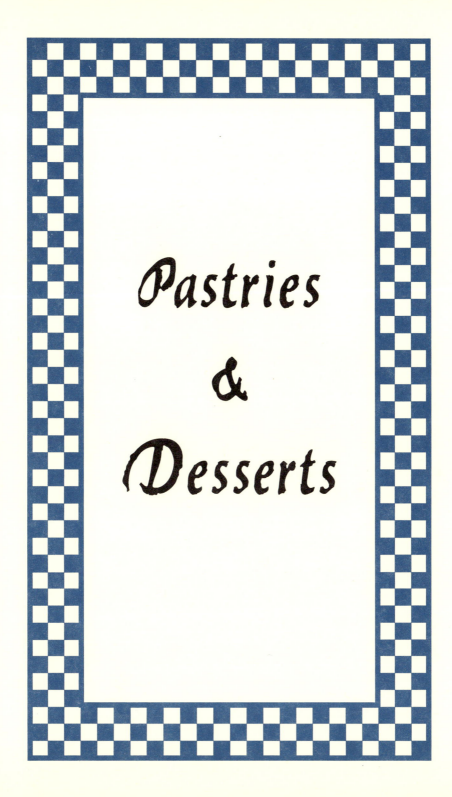

Pastries

&

Desserts

CANDY BAR PIE

6 chocolate bars with almonds (1.45 oz. each)
1-8 oz. container frozen whipped topping, thawed
1 T. vanilla

1 prepared graham cracker crust (8 or 9")
Shaved chocolate, opt.

In a double boiler or microwave oven, melt the chocolate bars. Quickly fold into the whipped topping. Stir in vanilla. Spoon into pie crust. Garnish with the shaved chocolate, if desired. Chill until ready to serve.

QUICK BLENDER CHERRY PIE

1 C. milk
2 T. margarine
¼ tsp. almond extract
2 eggs

½ C. baking mix (I use Bisquick)
¼ C. sugar
1 can cherry pie filling

Heat oven to 400°. Grease a 10" pie plate. Beat all the ingredients except pie filling and the Streusel topping that is listed below. Beat the mixture for 15 seconds in blender or 1 minute on high if you use hand beater. Pour into pie plate. Spoon the pie filling evenly over the top. Bake for 25 minutes. Top with the Streusel. Bake until streusel is brown or about 10 minutes longer. Cool; refrigerate any remaining pie. This is delicious served warm with vanilla ice cream.
STREUSEL TOPPING: Cut 2 tablespoons firm margarine into ½ cup baking mix, ½ cup brown sugar and ½ teaspoon ground cinnamon. Use fork to blend this until it is crumbly.
NOTE: This makes its own crust, so no pie shell is needed.

LEMONADE STAND PIE

1-6 oz. can frozen lemonade or pink lemonade concentrate, partially thawed
1 pt. vanilla ice cream (2 C.), softened

1-8 oz. tub whipped topping (I use Cool Whip), THAWED
1 prepared graham cracker crumb crust (9")

Beat concentrate in large mixer bowl with electric mixer on LOW speed about 30 SECONDS. Gradually spoon in ice cream; beat until well blended. Gently stir in whipped topping until smooth. If necessary, freeze until mixture will mound. Spoon into crust. Freeze for 4 hours or overnight until firm. Let stand at room temperature for 30 minutes or until pie can be cut easily.
NOTE: If you like you can garnish with strawberries. Store leftover pie in the freezer.

31

JIFFY PEANUT BUTTER PIE

1-8 oz. pkg. cream cheese
½ C. peanut butter
crust
2 C. whipped topping
(Cool Whip)

1 C. powdered sugar
1 prepared graham cracker

Blend cream cheese, peanut butter and powdered sugar until smooth. Fold in the Cool Whip. Pour into prepared crust. Refrigerate until firm enough to cut. (This can also be frozen, until needed). Drizzle chocolate syrup over the top of each piece of pie when you serve.

QUICK ICE CREAM PIE

1 qt. chocolate chip ice cream
1 prepared chocolate cookie
crust (9")

½ C. chocolate syrup

Spread softened ice cream into crust; pour chocolate syrup on top and swirl with knife. Cover and freeze until firm enough to cut.
WOW! Is this good!!!

UPSIDE-DOWN CHERRY PIE

1-21 oz. can cherry pie filling
1 T. butter or margarine
¾ C. flour

½ C. sugar
2 tsp. baking powder
½ C. milk

Pour pie filling into 10" deep-dish pie plate spread with 1 tablespoon margarine. Combine flour, sugar and baking powder in bowl; mix well. Stir in milk. Pour batter over pie filling. Bake at 350° for 20 minutes or until crust is brown. When pie is done, place on serving plate with pie filling side up. Makes 8 servings.

Love makes work a JOY, not a JOB.

CHOCO-PEANUT BUTTER MOUNDS

1-6 oz. pkg. semisweet
chocolate pieces
¼ C. creamy or chunky
peanut butter

2⅓ C. corn flakes
⅓ C. dry roasted peanuts

In 1-quart saucepan, stir together chocolate pieces and peanut butter. Cook over low heat until melted. Stir in corn flakes and nuts. Drop by teaspoonfuls onto waxed paper. Cool 15 to 20 minutes or until set. Makes about 32-1½" cookies.
NOTE: This is a very easy recipe for kids to make.

QUICK AND YUMMY KEY LIME PIE

20 butter cookies or vanilla
wafers
1-14 oz. can sweetened
condensed milk

¼ C. key lime juice
8 oz. whipped topping

Line 9" pie plate with whole cookies. Combine sweetened condensed milk and lime juice in bowl; mix well. Fold in whipped topping. Spoon into prepared pie plate. Freeze until firm. Makes 6 servings.

YOGURT PIE

1 graham cracker pie crust
(use the ones already made)
8 oz. yogurt, use your favorite
flavor (I like strawberry)

8 oz. whipped topping (I use
Cool Whip)

Combine the whipped topping with the yogurt. Fill the crust. Refrigerate at least 1 hour or until firm, before serving. If you like, top with fruit.

Kind words are like honey - sweet to the
taste and good for your health.

LITTLE FRUIT TARTS

This is very easy.

1-8¼ oz. can crushed
  pineapple, DRAINED
1-15 oz. can lemon pie filling
6 single-serve graham cracker
  crusts (1-4 oz. pkg.)

Assorted fresh or canned fruit
  such as berries, kiwi, peeled
  and sliced or mandarin
  oranges or bananas

Stir the lemon filling and pineapple together. Divide filling among crusts, allowing heaping ⅓ cup each. Arrange the fruit on top. Refrigerate until serving time.

EASY LEMON TART

1-15 oz. pkg. refrigerated
  ready-to-use pie crust
1 egg white

1 can lemon pie filling
½ C. powdered sugar
2 tsp. milk

Heat oven to 400°. Unfold the pastry dough for 1 crust and place on 12" pizza pan or cookie sheet. Spoon the lemon filling onto dough and spread to within ¾" of edge of pie dough. Brush EDGE with beaten egg white. Unfold and top with remaining pie crust. Press around the edge with finger to seal. Prick top surface with fork and brush with egg white. Bake 20 to 25 minutes or until lightly browned. Cook. With fork stir the powdered sugar and milk to make a smooth glaze. Drizzle on tart.

CREAMY CHERRY DESSERT

1 can cherry pie filling
1-14 oz. can sweetened
  condensed milk
1-8 oz. container whipped
  topping, thawed

1-15 oz. can crushed
  pineapple, DRAINED
1 C. MINIATURE marshmallows

In large bowl, combine all the ingredients. Stir until well blended. DO NOT BEAT, JUST GENTLY FOLD TOGETHER. CHILL.

QUICK CHOCOLATE MOUSSE

1-14 oz. can sweetened
 condensed milk
1-3.9 oz. pkg. instant
 chocolate pudding mix

1 C. cold water
1 C. whipping cream,
WHIPPED

In a large mixing bowl, combine milk, pudding mix and water. Beat until well mixed. Chill 5 minutes. Fold in whipped cream. Spoon into individual serving dishes. Garnish with additional whipped cream. Makes 4 to 6 servings.

INSTANT ICE CREAM

Makes 1 serving. Put ½ cup milk and 1 teaspoon vanilla and 1 tablespoon sugar in small Ziploc bag. Stir. Seal well. Place this bag into a gallon Ziploc bag that has been filled ¾ full with crushed ice with 6 tablespoons of table salt, sprinkled over the salt. Let it stay until ice cream has hardened. Shape gently once or twice during the freezing process. Do not put this in the freezer while this is hardening. This makes 1 serving and is very quick, easy and GOOD!!
NOTE: This is fun for kids to do.

FRIED APPLES

5 apples, peeled, thinly sliced
 (I use yellow delicious)
¼ C. melted margarine or
 butter

½ C. sugar
¼ tsp. cinnamon
¼ C. hot water

Place apple slices in melted margarine in skillet. Sprinkle with sugar and cinnamon. Pour hot water carefully down the side of skillet. Simmer, covered for 15 minutes or until apples are tender.

Some people are making such thorough preparations for rainy days that they aren't enjoying today's sunshine!

QUICK RICE PUDDING

4 C. milk
1 egg, beaten
1 pkg. (4 serving size)
  vanilla pudding mix (NOT
  INSTANT)
1 C. Minute rice

¼ tsp. cinnamon
¼ tsp. nutmeg
¼ C. raisins, opt.

Gradually stir milk and egg into pudding mix in saucepan. Add the rice and raisins. Stir over medium heat until mixture comes to a boil. Cook for 5 minutes, stirring once. Pour into dessert dishes. Sprinkle with cinnamon and nutmeg. Serve warm. If you like it cold, put it in refrigerator with plastic wrap on surface of pudding. Refrigerate for 1 hour.

BAKED PINEAPPLE CASSEROLE

¾ C. sugar
½ C. margarine, SOFTENED
4 eggs

1-20 oz. can crushed
  pineapple
5 slices bread, CUBED

Cream margarine and sugar in mixer bowl until light and fluffy. Beat in the eggs. Add the pineapple and bread cubes; mix well. Spoon into a greased baking dish. Bake at 350° for 45 minutes or until light brown. Makes 6 servings.

APPLE CRUNCH

1-21 oz. can apple pie filling
1 C. QUICK cooking oats
¼ C. margarine, softened

½ C. packed brown sugar
1 tsp. cinnamon
½ tsp. nutmeg

Spray loaf pan with non-stick baking spray. Spread the pie filling in loaf pan. Mix the oats, margarine, brown sugar, cinnamon and nutmeg in small bowl. Sprinkle over the pie filling. Bake at 325° for 30 minutes. Serve warm with vanilla ice cream or whipped topping.

HEAVENLY FRUIT DESSERT

16 oz. whipped topping (I use Cool-Whip)
8 oz. cream cheese, softened
2-20 oz. cans crushed pineapple, DRAINED, BUT SAVE JUICE

2-11 oz. cans mandarin oranges, DRAINED
2 C. miniature marshmallows
1 C. chopped pecans or English walnuts

Combine cream cheese and whipped topping in bowl; mix well until smooth. DRAIN pineapple, reserving ½ cup juice. Add pineapple, oranges and marshmallows to whipped topping mixture; mix well. Stir in pecans and reserved juice. Gently stir in until well mixed. Yields 15 servings.

LEMON DELIGHT

1 sm. pkg. lemon INSTANT pudding mix
1-6 oz. can crushed pineapple, DRAINED

1 angel food cake (purchase reg. already baked)

Prepare pudding using package directions. Stir in pineapple. Tear cake into bite size pieces. Fold into pineapple mixture. Spoon into shallow dish. Chill for 1 our or until firm. Yields 8 servings.
NOTE: You can use a different flavor pudding if you wish.

PECAN DESSERT

1 roll refrigerator sugar cookie dough
1-4 oz. pkg. butterscotch INSTANT pudding mix

¾ C. dark corn syrup
1 egg
1½ C. pecan halves

SLICE cookie dough ¼" thick. Press slices over the bottom and ¾" up the sides of a 9x13" baking pan. Mix pudding mix, corn syrup, milk and egg in bowl. Stir in pecans. Spoon into prepared pan on top of cookie dough. Bake at 350° for 30 to 35 minutes or until filling is SET. Cool completely. Cut into squares. Serve alone or with whipped topping. Makes 12 servings.

TWINKIE SURPRISE

1-10 oz. pkg. Twinkies
2-4 oz. pkgs. vanilla INSTANT
  pudding mix
3 C. milk

8 oz. whipped topping
2-1 oz. Heath bars, chopped

Cut Twinkies into halves lengthwise. Arrange cream side up in 9x13" pan or dish. Combine milk and pudding mix in bowl; beat until thick. Spread over Twinkies. Top with whipped topping and chopped Heath bars. Chill for 1 hour. Store in refrigerator. Makes 16 servings.

COTTAGE CHEESE DESSERT

1 lg. box any flavor jello (I like
  orange)
1 lg. can crushed pineapple
  and juice

1-24 oz. size cottage cheese
1 lb. size whipped topping (I
  use Cool Whip)

Mix together jello and pineapple. Add the cottage cheese and whipped topping. Mix together and refrigerate. Stir well and spoon into a serving dish.
NOTE: Even if you do not like cottage cheese, you'll like this dessert.

QUICK CINNAMON APPLE CAKE

Ready to serve in 40 minutes!!!

1 can apple pie filling
1 pkg. spice or yellow cake mix
3 eggs

4 T. sugar
1 tsp. ground cinnamon

Heat oven to 350°. Blend together the cake mix, apple filling and eggs in large mixer bowl. Beat at medium speed for 2 minutes. Combine sugar and cinnamon. Spread ½ the batter in greased 13x9" pan; sprinkle with ½ of the cinnamon and sugar. Repeat with remaining batter and cinnamon sugar. Bake 30 to 35 minutes, until wooden pick inserted in center of cake comes out clean. Cool. Serve with whipped topping.

VERY EASY CHEESECAKE

1 prepared graham
  cracker crust
2-8 oz. pkgs. cream cheese,
  softened
¾ C. sugar

3 eggs
1 tsp. vanilla
2 T. lemon juice
DASH of salt

Combine all the ingredients except the pie crust. Beat the eggs in, 1 at a time. Pour in unbaked graham cracker crust. Bake 30 to 35 minutes at 350°. CHILL AND SERVE WITH YOUR FAVORITE fruit topping. I use prepared pie filling. Cherry and blueberry are very good.

VERY EASY CHOCOLATE CAKE

1-4 oz. pkg. chocolate
  pudding mix (the
  cooked kind)

1 C. chocolate chips
1-2 layer pkg. chocolate
  cake mix

Cook pudding using package directions. Combine with dry cake mix in bowl; mix well. Pour into greased and floured 9x13" cake pan. Sprinkle with chocolate chips. Bake at 350° for 20 minutes. Makes 12 servings.

QUICK AND EASY FRUIT TURNOVERS

1 can refrigerated 8-count
  crescent dough
1-21 oz. can cherry pie filling
  or your favorite fruit filling

GLAZE:
½ C. powdered sugar
3 to 4 tsp. milk
Stir until smooth.

Heat oven to directions on can of dough. Separate dough triangles , lay out on cookie sheet. Place 2 or 3 teaspoons of filling in center of triangle of dough, keep it back from the edge of dough so it can be sealed. Lay a second triangle of dough over the first and crimp it with a fork. Bake according to directions on can of dough. Drizzle with powdered sugar glaze. Serve warm.

QUICK AND EASY FRUIT COBBLER

1 C. biscuit baking mix
1 can of your favorite
  fruit pie filling
¼ C. milk

⅓ C. sugar
2 T. margarine or butter
(If you like, you can add 1
  tsp. cinnamon to the biscuit
  mix)

Heat oven to 400°. Spray lightly a 9" baking pan with non-stick baking spray. Spoon the filling into the pan. Stir together biscuit mix, milk, sugar and margarine with fork until blended. Drop by spoonfuls on top of filling. Bake 20 to 25 minutes until golden brown. Serve warm.

VERY EASY PEACH COBBLER

1-29 oz. can sliced peaches
  (DO NOT DRAIN, USE JUICE
  AND PEACHES)

1-2 layer size pkg. yellow
  cake mix
1 stick margarine, sliced

Pour UNDRAINED peaches into buttered 9x13" baking dish. Sprinkle the cake mix over top. Dot with margarine. Bake at 350° for 35 minutes or until light brown. Serve warm with vanilla ice cream or whipped topping. Serves 10.

BISCUIT FRUIT DESSERT

½ C. sugar
2 cans fruit pie filling (use
  your favorite)
½ tsp. cinnamon

1-10 oz. can refrigerated
  flaky biscuits
¼ C. margarine or butter,
  MELTED

Heat oven to 400°. Pour the pie filling into a 13x9" pan. Combine the sugar and cinnamon in small bowl. Separate each biscuit into 2 sections; dip each section in margarine, then in cinnamon sugar. Arrange on top of filling. Bake 18 to 20 minutes, until golden brown. Serve warm with whipped topping or ice cream.

A Christian home is earths sweetest picture
of heaven.

SUPREME BLUEBERRY COBBLER

⅔ C. milk
¼ C. margarine or butter
1½ C. biscuit baking mix

1 C. sugar
1 can blueberry pie filling

Heat oven to 400°. Melt margarine in 11x7" baking dish. Add the milk, biscuit mix and sugar; stir until smooth. Drop blueberry filling by spoonfuls over batter. Bake 30 to 40 minutes or until golden brown. Serve with whipped topping or ice cream.

PEACH BREAD PUDDING

3 eggs
4 C. day old bread cubes
1½ C. milk
½ C. sugar

¼ tsp. almond extract
½ tsp. vanilla
1 can peach pie filling

Heat oven to 350°. Spread the bread cubes in greased 9" square pan. Whisk together the eggs, milk, sugar and flavorings. Stir in 1 cup peach filling. Pour this over the bread cubes, pressing custard down in bread with back of spoon. Bake 30 to 40 minutes or until knife comes out clean. Heat remaining peach filling and spoon over warm pudding.

PEACH CRISP

2 cans peach pie filling
¼ C. flour
¼ C. quick oatmeal
¼ C. brown sugar

¾ tsp. ground cinnamon
2 T. butter or margarine
¼ C. chopped pecans, opt.

Heat oven to 400°. Pour peach pie filling into a shallow 1½-quart casserole. In a small bowl, mix the oats, flour, brown sugar, cinnamon and nuts. Cut in butter until mixture is crumbly. Sprinkle over filling. Bake 25 minutes or until topping is golden brown. Cool. Serve with ice cream or whipped topping (I use Cool Whip).

*Every Christian occupies some kind of a pulpit
and sends out some kind of sermon everyday.*

FRUIT COOKIE PIZZA

½ pkg. (20 oz.) refrigerated
  sugar cookie dough (save
  remainder to bake for cookies)
1-12 oz. pkg. cream cheese,
  SOFTENED

¼ C. powdered sugar
1 can strawberry pie filling or
  your favorite fruit pie filling)*

*NOTE: You can also use fresh fruit instead of the pie filling.

Heat oven to 350°. Pat out cookie dough to 10 inch circle on greased cookie sheet. Bake 7 to 9 minutes until golden brown. Cool. Stir powdered sugar into cream cheese. Spread over cookie dough to within ½" of edge. Spoon strawberry filling or fresh fruit over cream cheese. Cut into wedges just like when you serve pizza.

MICROWAVE S'MORES

4 graham crackers, broken
  into broken halves

2 milk chocolate bars,
  into halves
4 lg. marshmallows

Place 1 graham cracker ½ on paper towel; top with chocolate bar ½ and marshmallow. Microwave at HIGH (100%) 10 to 15 SECONDS or just until marshmallow begins to puff. Immediately top with second graham cracker ½. Gently press together. Repeat for EACH serving. Serve at once.

QUICK ONE-BOWL BROWNIES

4 sqs. unsweetened chocolate
¾ C. (1½ sticks) margarine or
  butter
2 C. sugar
3 eggs

1 tsp. vanilla
1 C. flour
1½ C. chopped walnuts or
  pecans

Heat oven to 350°. MICROWAVE chocolate and margarine in large microwaveable bowl on HIGH for 2 minutes or until margarine is melted. STIR UNTIL CHOCOLATE IS COMPLETELY MELTED. STIR sugar into chocolate until well blended. Stir in eggs and vanilla until completely mixed. Mix in flour until well blended. Stir in nuts. SPREAD in greased 13x9" pan. Bake for 30 to 35 minutes or until toothpick inserted into center comes out with fudgy crumbs. DO NOT OVERBAKE!!! COOL, THEN CUT INTO SQUARES.

QUICK CHOCOLATE COOKIES

1-2 layer size pkg. chocolate
   cake mix
2 eggs
1 C. Miracle Whip dressing

1 C. semisweet chocolate
   chips
½ C. chopped walnuts or
   pecans

Mix cake mix, eggs and dressing in large bowl with electric mixer on medium speed until blended. Stir in remaining ingredients. Drop rounded teaspoonfuls onto greased cookie sheets. Bake at 350° for 10 to 12 minutes or until edges are lightly browned. Makes 4 dozen.

LOW-FAT BROWNIES

1 pkg. fudge brownie mix
2 egg whites

⅓ C. (8 oz.) nonfat plain
   yogurt
1 tsp. vanilla

Preheat oven to 350°. Grease bottom only of 13x9x2" pan. Combine brownie mix, egg whites, yogurt and vanilla extract in large bowl. Stir with spoon until well blended. (Batter will be stiff). Spread in pan. Bake at 350° for 22 minutes or until set. Cool completely.

EASY PUDDING COOKIES

1 C. baking mix (I use Bisquick)
1 pkg. favorite INSTANT
   pudding mix (3½ or
   4½ size)

¼ C. salad oil
1 egg

Heat oven to 350°. Mix all the ingredients until the dough forms a ball. Shape dough into balls, using 1 teaspoon of dough for each cookie. Place on UNGREASED cookie sheet. Grease the bottom of glass and then dip it in sugar. Press on the balls to flatten them. Bake for 8 minutes.
NOTE: This is a great cookie for your kids to make or just when you are in a big hurry.

QUICK APPLE-CINNAMON ROLLS

⅓ C. chopped pecans
¼ C. firmly packed brown
  sugar

1-11 oz. can refrigerated
  cinnamon raisin Danish rolls
1-21 oz. can apple pie filling,
  divided

Spray a 9" pan with a non-stick baking spray. Combine 1 cup apple pie filling, pecans and sugar; spread in pan. Arrange rolls on top of apple mixture. Bake in 375° oven for 10 minutes or until light brown. Invert onto serving plate immediately. Top with the remaining apple pie filling when served.

QUICK AND EASY FUDGE

2 T. butter
1½ C. sugar
⅔ C. evaporated milk
¼ tsp. salt
2 C. (4 oz.) mini-marshmallows

1½ C. (9 oz.) semisweet
  chocolate chips
1 C. chopped walnuts or
  pecans
1 tsp. vanilla

Bring butter, sugar, evaporated milk and salt to a boil in medium-size, heavy saucepan, over medium heat, stirring constantly. Boil for 4 or 5 minutes, stirring constantly. Remove from heat. Stir in marshmallows, chocolate chips, nuts and vanilla. Stir vigorously for 1 minute or until marshmallows are melted. Pour into foil-lined 8" square pan. Sprinkle with nuts if desired. CHILL until firm. Cut into squares.

CHOCOLATE COVERED
MARSHMALLOWS

1 lb. semisweet chocolate

1 bag of lg. marshmallows

Dip marshmallows, 1 by 1, into very well melted chocolate. Drain well. Store where it is cool. Very good and very quick.

All people smile in the same language.

FRUIT DIP

1-8 oz. pkg. cream cheese,
  softened

1-8 oz. container strawberry
  or any flavor yogurt

Mix cream cheese with electric mixer on medium speed until smooth. Add the yogurt; mix until well blended. SERVE WITH ASSORTED FRESH FRUIT.

MARSHMALLOW DIP AND FRUIT

1-7 oz. jar marshmallow creme
3 oz. cream cheese, SOFTENED
Strawberries, stemmed and
  washed, (leave whole)

Red and yellow Delicious
  apples, cored, sliced
  (I leave peel on)

Combine the marshmallow cream and cream cheese with electric mixer until smooth. Serve with the above fruit (or fruit of your choice) as a dip. Store any leftover in the refrigerator.

True friends are like diamonds,
precious but rare.
False friends are like autumn leaves,
found everywhere.

Write Extra Recipes Here

Vegetables

&

Miscellaneous

YUMMY POTATO OVEN SLICES

1.1 oz. pkg. Hidden Valley
  Ranch Italian salad dressing
  mix
¾ C. grated Parmesan
  cheese
⅓ C. butter or margarine,
  melted

4 med. potatoes, sliced ¼"
  thick about 2½ lbs.
  (SCRUB THE POTATOES, BUT
  DO NOT PEEL)

Preheat oven to 400°. In small bowl, combine salad dressing mix and cheese. Brush 2 shallow baking pans with some of the butter. Place potato slices in pans in SINGLE layer. Brush generously with the remaining butter; then sprinkle evenly with dressing mixture. Bake until golden brown and tender. It usually takes about 20 minutes.

EASY SKILLET BAKED BEANS

3 slices bacon, cut into
  1" pieces
1 med. onion, chopped

¼ C. chili sauce
1 tsp. prepared mustard
2-16 oz. cans pork and
  beans (about ½ C.)

Cook and stir bacon and onion in 10" skillet until bacon is crisp. Stir in remaining ingredinets. Heat to boiling; reduce heat. Simmer uncovered, stirring occasioanlly, until all liquid is absorbed, ususaly about 15 minutes.

IMPOSSIBLE BROCCOLI PIE

2-10 oz. pkgs. frozen
  chopped broccoli
3 C. shredded Cheddar
  cheese (12 oz.)
⅔ C. chopped onion
1⅓ C . milk

3 eggs
¾ C. Bisquick
¾ tsp. salt
¼ tsp. pepper

Heat oven to 400°. Grease pie plate (large). Rinse broccoli under cold water to thaw; drain thoroughly. Mix broccoli, 2 cups of the cheese and the onion in the pie plate. Beat milk, eggs, baking mix, salt and pepper until smooth, 1 minute with hand beater. Pour into pie plate. Bake until knife inserted in center comes out clean, 25 to 35 minutes. Top with remaining cheese. Bake just until cheese is melted, 1 to 2 minutes longer. Let stand for 5 minutes before serving.

HERB ROASTED POTATOES

½ C. Miracle Whip
1 T. each: dried rosemary,
  garlic powder and onion
  powder
1 tsp. seasoned salt

1 T. water
2 lbs. small RED potatoes,
  washed and quartered

Mix the dressing, seasonings and water in large bowl. Add the potatoes, toss to coat. Place potatoes on greased cookie sheet. Bake at 400° for 30 to 40 minutes or until golden brown, stirring after 15 minutes.

CHEESY VEGETABLES

1-10¾ oz. can condensed
  golden corn soup
½ C. milk

1-16 oz. bag frozen mixture
  of broccoli, cauliflower and
  carrots
½ C. shredded Cheddar
  cheese

In a saucepan, mix soup, milk and vegetables. Over medium heat, heat to a boil. Cover and cook over low heat for 15 minutes or until vegetables are tender. Stir in cheese and heat until cheese is melted.

POTATO PATTIES

2 C. mashed potatoes (use
  instant if you like to save time,
  they taste very good)
1 egg, lightly beaten

2 T. flour
¼ C. pkgd. seasoned bread
  crumbs

Mix all the ingredients well. Shape into patties ½" thick. Cook in a sprayed non-stick skillet for 2 minutes on each side or until golden brown.
NOTE: Everyone loves these, young and old alike.

A hug is a perfect gift - one size fits all
and nobody minds if you give it back.

GREEN BEAN CASSEROLE

2 med. size cans green beans, drained
1 C. condensed cream of msuhroom soup

1-4 oz. pkg. sliced almonds
1-4 oz. can water chestnuts, sliced
2 C. cheese crackers, crushed

LIGHTLY mix the beans, soup, almonds and water chestnuts in a medium bowl. Spray a 2-quart casserole with non-stick baking spray. Place the bean mixture in the casserole and top with crushed cheese crackers. Bake at 350° for 25 minutes. Serves 8.

NO-FRY FRENCH FRIES

4 lg. potatoes
5 tsp. vegetable oil

½ tsp. pepper
½ tsp. salt

Preheat oven to 425°. Wash potatoes and cut out bad spots. Slice UNPEELED POTATOES into French fries. Place in a bowl of water and ice cubes. Chill for 10 minutes. Put oil, salt and pepper in 9" square baking dish. Heat pan in oven. Dry potatoes on paper towels and place in pan. Turn potatoes over to coat with oil and seasonings. BAke for 30 minutes until crisp and lightly browned. NOTE: A GOOD VARIATION IS TO SPRINKLE WITH PARMESAN CHEESE 5 MINUTES BEFORE DONE!!

CHEESY RICE CASSEROLE

2 C. hot, cooked rice (NOT Minute rice)
1⅓ C. (2.8 oz. can) French fried onions

1 C. sour cream
16 oz. jar med. salsa
1 C. shredded Cheddar cheese

Mix the rice and ⅔ cup French fried onions; spoon ½ the rice in 2-quart microwave dish. Top with sour cream. Spoon ½ the salsa and cheese on top. Cover with remaining rice, salsa and cheese. Cover, microwave 8 minutes or until hot. Top with ⅔ cup onions. Microwave 1 minute. Serve.

EASY WESTERN BAKED BEANS

1 lb. ground beef
1 med. onion, chopped
¼ C. catsup
1 T. prepared mustard

1 tsp. salt
2 T. brown sugar
2-16 oz. cans pork and
    beans (your favorite brand)

BROWN GROUND BEEF AND ONION IN OIL; DRAIN. Mix with other ingreidents. Place in 2-quart baking dish. Bake in 325° oven for 35 minutes. Spray your baking dish with non-stick spray.

BROCCOLI CASSEROLE

2-10 oz. pkgs. frozen chopped
    broccoli
1 C. grated Cheddar cheese
1 C. mayonnaise

2 eggs
1 can condensed cream of
    mushroom soup

Cook broccoli per package directions, with salt and pepper. DRAIN. Combine remaining ingredients and fold in broccoli. Bake at 350° for 45 minutes. Makes 8 servings.

VEGETABLE PASTA

12 oz. uncooked fettcuccini
    or your favorite long pasta
1-16 oz. frozen cauliflower,
    carrots and snow pea pods

⅓ C. creamy Caesar, Italian
    or ranch salad dressing
1 tsp. dried basil
1 tsp. dried garlic powder
⅓ C. grated Parmesan
    cheese

Cook pasta according to package directions; drain. Cook vegetables according to package directions. Combine pasta, vegetables, dressing and spices in large skillet, mix well. Cook over medium heat just until heated through. Add the cheese, toss to coat the pasta. Add salt and pepper to taste.

Country Parson -
"You ought to think as kindly about
a fellow today as you likely will at his funeral".

MICROWAVE SAUTEED MUSHROOMS

½ lb. fresh mushrooms   ⅓ C. butter or margarine
1 clove garlic, minced

Clean the mushrooms and slice. Put in an 8" round dish. Add the garlic and butter. Cook, COVERED, at HIGH for 6 ot 7 minutes. Serve with any meal or as a topping for steak.

PICKLED BEETS

1 C. sugar and enough apple cider VINEGAR to dissolve the sugar. Mix this thoroughly. Add 2 cans of DRAINED BEETS. ADD more vinegar to BARELY cover the beets. Place in covered jar and place in the refrigerator. Very Good!!

CORN FRITTERS

½ C. COLD water   1 egg
2 C. baking mix (I use Bisquick)   1 lb. 1 oz. whole kernel corn,
                               DRAINED (about 2 C.)

Heat vegetable oil (2 to3") in Dutch oven or a deep fryer to 375°. In small bowl mix the baking mix, water and egg with a fork until it smooth. Stir in corn, DO NOT BEAT! Drop the batter by tablespoons into the heated oil. Turn and fry until they are golden brown. DRAIN ON PAPER TOWELS. SERVE WARM WITH MAPLE SYRUP. (Heat the syrup too). Be prepared for them to ask for seconds!

EGG SALAD FILLING

4 eggs, hard cooked, finely   2 T. mayonnaise
  chopped   ¼ tsp. celery salt
¼ C. finely chopped celery   1½ tsp. sugar
1 T. prepared mustard   1 T. parsley flakes

Combine the ingredients and mix thoroughly. Makes enough filling for 4 to 6 sandwiches. Use your favorite bread.

HOT HAM AND CHEESE SANDWICH

12 slices crisp fried bacon
12-1 oz. slices cooked chicken
  breast
12 slices tomato

6 English muffins, split
2 C. cheese sauce

Layer 2 slices bacon, 1 slice chicken and 1 slice tomato on each muffin half. Heat cheese sauce in saucepan until bubbly. Spoon over the tomato. Serve at once.

MEXICAN CHICKEN AND CHEESE SANDWICH

2 slices sourdough or other
  FIRM slices bread
2 slices cheese slices (I like
  Velveeta)
1 T. salsa

2 to 3 oz. cooked chicken
Soft butter or margarine

Top 1 bread slice with 1 slice of cheese, salsa, chicken, second slice of cheese and second bread slice. Spread sandwich with butter or margarine. Grill over medium low heat until lightly browned on both sides. Makes 1 sandwich.
NOTE: This is good with leftover turkey too!!!

PAN GRAVY

2 T. meat drippings (fat and
  juices)
2 T. flour

1 C. liquid (meat juices,
  broth, water)
Salt and pepper to taste

Place meat on warm platter; keep warm while preparing gravy. POur drippings from pan into bowl, leaving brown particles in pan. Return 2 tablespoons drippings to pan. Measure accurately because too little fat makes gravy lumpy. Stir in flour (measure accurately so gravy is not greasy). Cook over low heat, stirring constantly, until mixture is smooth and bubbly; remove from heat. Stir in liquid. Heat to boiling, stirring constantly. Boil and stir for 1 minute. Stir in few drops browning sauce if desired for a deeper color. Sprinkle with salt and pepper.

BASIC WHITE SAUCE
(MICROWAVE)

1 C. milk
2 T. butter or margarine

2 T. flour
¼ tsp. salt

In a medium size bowl, melt the butter or margarine. Add the flour and salt. Gradually add milk; stir until smooth. Cook at MEDIUM (microwave) for 5 to 6 minutes or until sauce is thickened. Stir occasioanlly while cooking.
NOTE: If you want a quick cheese sauce, just add ¾ cup shredded cheese (your favorite). Just heat until cheese melts after cooking.

Give me a pure heart
That I may see thee,
A humble heart
That I may hear thee,
A heart of love
That I may serve thee,
A heart of faith
That I may abide in thee.

Write Extra Recipes Here

INDEX

APPETIZERS & BEVERAGES

BREADS & BREAKFAST

i

MAIN ENTREES & CASSEROLES

SOUP & SALADS

PASTRIES & DESSERTS

VEGETABLES & MISCELLANEOUS

VEGETABLES & MISCELLANEOUS

HANDY CHART OF KITCHEN MATH WITH METRIC

KITCHEN MATH WITH METRIC TABLES

Measure	Equivalent	Metric (ML)
1 tablespoon	3 teaspoons	14.8 milliliters
2 tablespoons	1 ounce	29.6 milliliters
1 jigger	1½ ounces	44.4 milliliters
¼ cup	4 tablespoons	59.2 milliliters
⅓ cup	5 tablespoons plus 1 teaspoon	78.9 milliliters
½ cup	8 tablespoons	118.4 milliliters
1 cup	16 tablespoons	236.8 milliliters
1 pint	2 cups	473.6 milliliters
1 quart	4 cups	947.2 milliliters
1 liter	4 cups plus 3 tablespoons	1.000.0 milliliters
1 ounce (dry)	2 tablespoons	28.35 grams
1 pound	16 ounces	453.59 grams
2.21 pounds	35.3 ounces	1.00 kilogram

THE APPROXIMATE CONVERSION FACTORS
FOR UNITS OF VOLUME

To Convert from	To	Multiply by
teaspoons (tsp.)	milliliters (ml)	5
tablespoons (T.)	milliliters (ml)	15
fluid ounces (fl. oz.)	milliliters (ml)	30
cups (C.)	liters (l)	0.24
pints (pt.)	liters (l)	0.47
quarts (qt.)	liters (l)	0.95
gallons (gal.)	liters (l)	3.8
cubic feet (ft^3)	cubic meters (m^3)	0.03
cubic yards (yd^3)	cubic meters (m^3)	0.76
milliliters (ml)	fluid ounces (fl. oz.)	0.03
liters (l)	pints (pt.)	2.1
liters (l)	quarts (qt.)	1.06
liters (l)	gallons (gal.)	0.26
cubic meters (m^3)	cubic feet (ft^3)	35
cubic meters (m^3)	cubic yards (yd^3)	1.3

SIMPLIFIED MEASURES

dash = less than ⅛ tsp.

3 tsp. = 1 T.

16 T. = 1 C.

1 C. = ½ pt.

2 C. = 1 pt.

2 pts. (4 C.) = 1 qt.

4 qts. (liquid) = 1 gal.

8 qts. (solid) = 1 peck

4 pecks = 1 bushel

16 oz. = 1 lb.

If you want to measure part-cups by the tablespoon, remember:

4 T. = ¼ C.

5⅓ T. = ⅓ C.

8 T. = ½ C.

10⅔ T. = ⅔ C.

12 T. = ¾ C.

14 T. = ⅞ C.

CONTENTS OF CANS

Of the different sizes of cans used by commercial canners, the most common are:

Size	Average Contents
8 ounces	1 cup
picnic	1¼ cups
No. 300	1¾ cups
No. 1 tall	2 cups
No. 303	2 cups
No. 2	2½ cups
No. 2½	3½ cups
No. 3	4 cups
No. 10	12 to 13 cups

OVEN TEMPERATURES

Slow	300°
Slow moderate	325°
Moderate	350°
Quick moderate	375°
Moderately hot	400°
Hot	425°
Very hot	475°

DEEP-FAT FRYING TEMPERATURES WITHOUT A THERMOMETER

A 1-inch cube of white bread will turn golden brown:

345° to 355°	65 seconds
355° to 365°	60 seconds
365° to 375°	50 seconds
375° to 385°	40 seconds
385° to 395°	20 seconds

SUBSTITUTIONS

FOR:	YOU CAN USE:
1 T. cornstarch	2 T. flour OR 1½ T. quick cooking tapioca
1 C. cake flour	1 C. less 2 T. all-purpose flour
1 C. all-purpose flour	1 C. plus 2 T. cake flour
1 square chocolate	3 T. cocoa and 1 T. fat
1 C. melted shortening	1 C. salad oil (may not be substituted for solid shortening)
1 C. milk	½ C. evaporated milk and ½ C. water
1 C. sour milk or buttermilk	1 T. lemon juice or vinegar and enough sweet milk to measure 1 C.
1 C. heavy cream	⅔ C. milk and ⅓ C. butter
1 C. heavy cream, whipped	⅔ C. well-chilled evaporated milk, whipped
Sweetened condensed milk	No substitution
1 egg	2 T. dried whole egg and 2 T. water
1 tsp. baking powder	¼ tsp. baking soda and 1 tsp. cream of tartar OR ¼ tsp. baking soda and ½ C. sour milk, buttermilk or molasses; reduce other liquid ½ C.
1 C. sugar	1 C. honey; reduce other liquid ¼ C.; reduce baking temperature 25°
1 C. miniature marshmallows	About 10 large marshmallows, cut up
1 medium onion (2½ dia.)	2 T. instant minced onion OR 1 tsp. onion powder OR 2 tsp. onion salt; reduce salt 1 tsp.
1 garlic clove	⅛ tsp. garlic powder OR ¼ tsp. garlic salt; reduce salt ⅛ tsp.
1 T. fresh herbs	1 tsp. dried herbs OR ¼ tsp. powdered herbs OR ½ tsp. herb salt; reduce salt ¼ tsp.

COMMON CAUSES OF FAILURE IN BAKING

BISCUITS
1. Rough biscuits caused from insufficient mixing.
2. Dry biscuits caused from baking in too slow an oven and handling too much.
3. Uneven browning caused from cooking in dark surface pan (use a cookie sheet or shallow bright finish pan), too high a temperature and rolling the dough too thin.

MUFFINS
1. Coarse texture caused from insufficient stirring and cooking at too low a temperature.
2. Tunnels in muffins, peaks in center and soggy texture are caused from overmixing.
3. For a nice muffin, mix well but light and bake at correct temperature.

CAKES
1. Cracks and uneven surface may be caused by too much flour, too hot an oven and sometimes from cold oven start.
2. Cake is dry may be caused by too much flour, too little shortening, too much baking powder or cooking at too low a temperature.
3. A heavy cake means too much sugar has been used or baked too short a period.
4. A sticky crust is caused by too much sugar.
5. Coarse grained cake may be caused by too little mixing, too much fat, too much baking powder, using fat too soft, and baking at too low a temperature.
6. Cakes fall may be caused by using insufficient flour, under baking, too much sugar, too much fat or not enough baking powder.
7. Uneven browning may be caused from cooking cakes at too high a temperature, crowding the shelf (allow at least 2" around pans) or using dark pans (use bright finish, smooth bottomed pans).
8. Cake has uneven color is caused from not mixing well. Mix thoroughly, but do not over mix.

PIES
1. Pastry crumbles caused by overmixing flour and fat.
2. Pastry is tough caused by using too much water and over mixing dough.
3. Pies do not burn - for fruit or custard pies use a Pyrex pie pan or an enamel pan and bake at 400° to 425° constant temperature.

BREADS (YEAST)
1. Yeast bread is porous - this is caused by over-rising or cooking at too low a temperature.
2. Crust is dark and blisters - this is caused by under-rising, the bread will blister just under the crust.
3. Bread does not rise - this is caused from over-kneading or from using old yeast.
4. Bread is streaked - this is caused from underkneading and not kneading evenly.
5. Bread baked uneven - caused by using old dark pans, too much dough in pan, crowding the oven shelf or cooking at too high a temperature.

BEEF

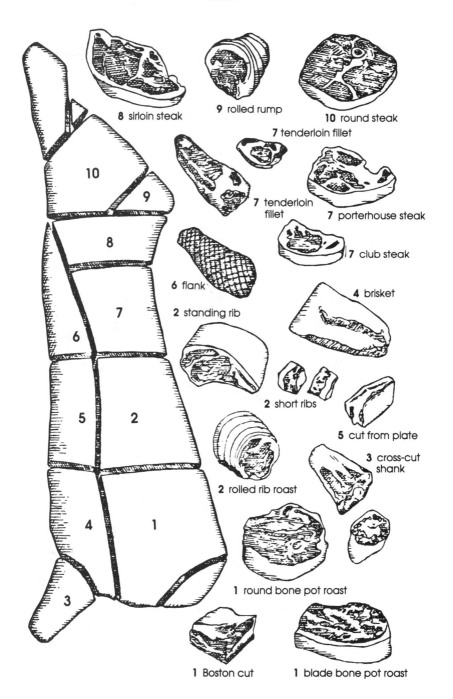

8 sirloin steak

9 rolled rump

10 round steak

7 tenderloin fillet

7 tenderloin fillet

7 porterhouse steak

7 club steak

6 flank

2 standing rib

4 brisket

2 short ribs

5 cut from plate

3 cross-cut shank

2 rolled rib roast

1 round bone pot roast

1 Boston cut

1 blade bone pot roast

VEAL

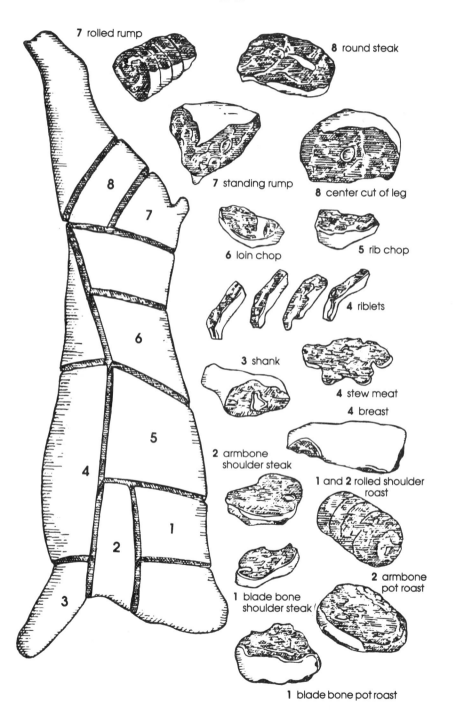

7 rolled rump

8 round steak

7 standing rump

8 center cut of leg

6 loin chop

5 rib chop

4 riblets

3 shank

4 stew meat

4 breast

2 armbone
shoulder steak

1 and 2 rolled shoulder
roast

1 blade bone
shoulder steak

2 armbone
pot roast

1 blade bone pot roast

PORK

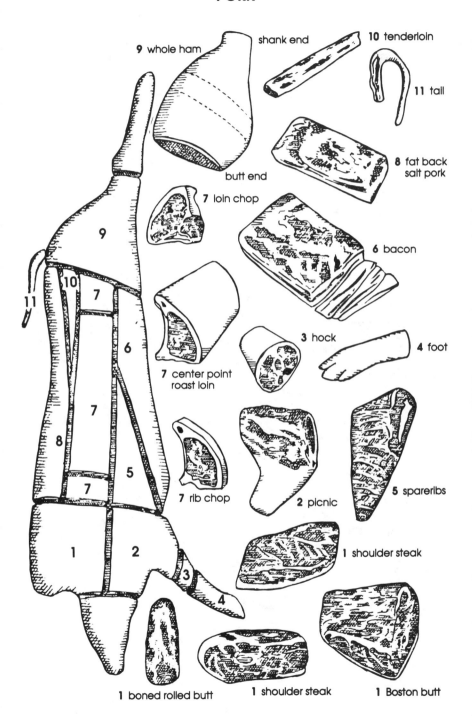

9 whole ham
shank end
10 tenderloin
11 tail
8 fat back salt pork
butt end
7 loin chop
6 bacon
9
10
7
11
6
7 center point roast loin
3 hock
4 foot
7
8
5
7
7 rib chop
2 picnic
5 spareribs
1
2
3
4
1 shoulder steak
1 boned rolled butt
1 shoulder steak
1 Boston butt

LAMB

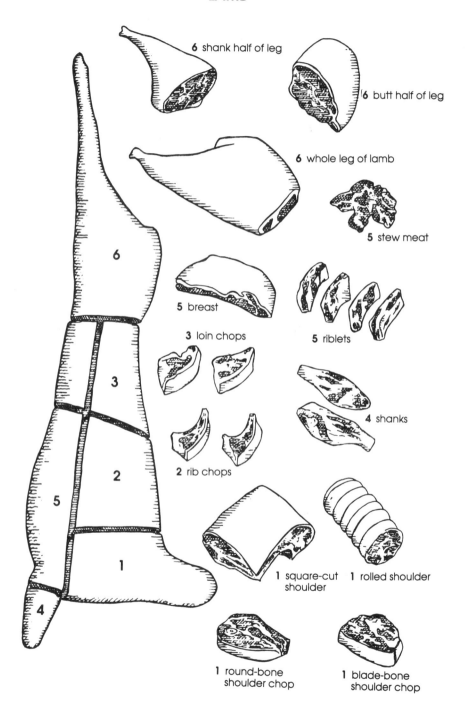

6 shank half of leg

6 butt half of leg

6 whole leg of lamb

5 stew meat

6

5 breast

5 riblets

3 loin chops

2 rib chops

4 shanks

3

2

5

1

4

1 square-cut shoulder

1 rolled shoulder

1 round-bone shoulder chop

1 blade-bone shoulder chop

HOUSEHOLD HINTS

TABLE OF CONTENTS

INDEX

I. THE KITCHEN

GENERAL

Salt
1. If stew is too salty, add raw cut potatoes and discard once they have cooked and absorbed the salt. Another remedy is to add a teaspoon each of cider vinegar and sugar. Or, simply add sugar.

2. If soup or stew is too sweet, add salt. For a main dish or vegetable, add a teaspoon of cider vinegar.

Gravy
3. For pale gravy, color with a few drops of Kitchen Bouquet. Or to avoid the problem in the first place, brown the flour well before adding the liquid. This also helps prevent lumpy gravy.

4. To make gravy smooth, keep a jar with a mixture of equal parts of flour and cornstarch. Put 3 or 4 tablespoons of this mixture in another jar and add some water. Shake, and in a few minutes you will have a smooth paste for gravy.

5. To remedy greasy gravy, add a small amount of baking soda.

6. For quick thickener for gravies, add some instant potatoes to your gravy and it will thicken beautifully.

Vegetables
7. If fresh vegetables are wilted or blemished, pick off the brown edges. Sprinkle with cool water, wrap in towel and refrigerate for an hour or so.

8. Perk up soggy lettuce by adding lemon juice to a bowl of cold water and soak for an hour in the refrigerator.

9. Lettuce and celery will crisp up fast if you place it in a pan of cold water and add a few sliced potatoes.

10. If vegetables are overdone, put the pot in a pan of cold water. Let it stand from 15 minutes to 1/2 hour without scraping pan.

11. By lining the crisper section of your refrigerator with newspaper and wrapping vegetables with it, moisture will be absorbed and your vegetables will stay fresher longer.

12. Store leftover corn, peas, green beans, carrots, celery, potatoes and onions in a container in the freezer. Add to other ingredients when making stew.

13. To keep the flavor in the vegetables, add a small amount of sugar to the water after cooking carrots, peas, beets, and corn.

14. Onions, broccoli and Brussels sprouts will cook faster if you make an X-shaped cut at the base of the vegetable.

Eggs
15. If you shake the egg and you hear a rattle, you can be sure it's stale. A really fresh egg will sink and a stale one will float.

16. If you are making deviled eggs and want to slice it perfectly, dip the knife in water first. The slice will be smooth with no yolk sticking to the knife.

17. The white of an egg is easiest to beat when it's at room temperature. So leave it out of the refrigerator about a half an hour before using it.

18. To make light and fluffy scrambled eggs, add a little water while beating the eggs.

19. Add vinegar to the water while boiling eggs. Vinegar helps to seal the egg, since it acts on the calcium in the shell.

20. STORING EGGS: 1. Place your eggs in those tight-sealing egg containers and they will last longer in the refrigerator. You really shouldn't keep eggs longer than 11 days. 2. Cover them with oil on the top in a sealed container in the refrigerator. 3. For long term storage: If there's a special on eggs at your local supermarket, you can take advantage of it. Just crack all the eggs open and put them in the freezer unit. To use one egg at a time, put single eggs in the ice tray. When frozen, put the egg cubes in a sealed plastic bag. You can take out the cubes one at a time for daily use. If you use eggs in twos or threes, freeze them that way in a plastic sack.

21. To make quick-diced eggs, take your potato masher and go to work on a boiled egg.

22. If you wrap each egg in aluminum foil before boiling it, the shell won't crack when it's boiling.

23. To make those eggs go further when making scrambled eggs for a crowd, add a pinch of baking powder and 2 teaspoons of water per egg.

24. A great trick for peeling eggs the easy way. When they are finished boiling, turn off the heat and just let them sit in the pan with the lid on for about 5 minutes. Steam will build up under the shell and they will just fall away.

25. Or, quickly rinse hot hard-boiled eggs in cold water, and the shells will be easier to remove.

26. When you have saved a lot of egg yolks from previous recipes, use them in place of whole eggs for baking or thickening. Just add 2 yolks for every whole egg.

27. Fresh or hard-boiled? Spin the egg. If it wobbles, it is raw - if it spins easily, it's hard boiled.

28. Add a few drops of vinegar to the water when poaching an egg to keep it from running all over the pan.

29. Add 1 tablespoon of water per egg white to increase the quantity of beaten egg white when making meringue.

30. Try adding eggshells to coffee after it has perked, for a better flavor.

31. Fresh eggs are rough and chalky in appearance. Old eggs are smooth and shiny.

32. Pierce the end of an egg with a pin, and it will not break when placed in boiling water.

33. Beaten egg whites will be more stable if you add 1 teaspoon cream of tartar to each cup of egg whites (7 or 8 eggs).

34. A small funnel is handy for separating egg whites from yolks. Open the egg over the funnel and the white will run through and the yolk will remain.

35. For baking, it's best to use medium to large eggs. Extra large may cause cakes to fall when cooled.

36. Brown and white shells are the same quality.

37. Egg whites can be kept up to 1 year. Add them to a plastic container as you "collect them" for use in meringues, angel food cake . . . 1 cup equals 7 or 8 egg whites. You can also refreeze defrosted egg whites.

38. For fluffier omelets, add a pinch of cornstarch before beating.

Potatoes

39. Overcooked potatoes can become soggy when the milk is added. Sprinkle with dry powdered milk for the fluffiest mashed potatoes ever.

40. To hurry up baked potatoes, boil in salted water for 10 minutes, then place in a very hot oven. Or, cut potatoes in half and place them face down on a baking sheet in the oven to make the baking time shorter.

41. When making potato pancakes, add a little sour cream to keep potatoes from discoloring.

42. Save some of the water in which the potatoes were boiled - add to some powdered milk and use when mashing. This restores some of the nutrients that were lost in the cooking process.

43. Use a couple of tablespoons of cream cheese in place of butter for your potatoes; try using sour cream instead of milk when mashing.

Onions

44. To avoid tears when peeling onions, peel them under cold water or refrigerate before chopping.

45. For sandwiches to go in lunchboxes, sprinkle with dried onion. They will have turned into crisp pieces by lunchtime.

46. Peel and quarter onions. Place 1 layer deep in a pan and freeze. Quickly pack in bags or containers while frozen. Use as needed, chopping onions while frozen, with a sharp knife.

Tomatoes
47. Keep tomatoes in storage with stems pointed downward and they will retain their freshness longer.
48. Sunlight doesn't ripen tomatoes. It's the warmth that makes them ripen. So find a warm spot near the stove or dishwasher where they can get a little heat.
49. Save the juice from canned tomatoes in ice cube trays. When frozen, store in plastic bags in freezer for cooking use or for tomato drinks.
50. To improve the flavor of inexpensive tomato juice, pour a 46-ounce can of it into a refrigerator jar and add 1 chopped green onion and a cut-up stalk of celery.

A quick way to whip cream
51. A pinch of salt added to the cream before whipping strengthens the fat cells and makes them more elastic. This helps the cream stiffen much more quickly.

Cream that will not whip
52. Chill cream, bowl and beater well. Set bowl of cream into a bowl of ice water while you're whipping. Add the white of an egg. Chill and then whip. If the cream still does not stiffen, gradually whip in 3 or 4 drops of lemon juice. Cream whipped ahead of time will not separate if you add a touch of unflavored gelatin (¼ teaspoon per cup of cream). To eliminate a lot of mess when whipping cream with an electric beater, try this: Cut 2 holes in the middle of a piece of waxed paper, then slip the stems of the beaters through the holes and attach the beaters to the machine. Simply place paper and beaters over the bowl and whip away.

Rock-hard brown sugar
53. Add a slice of soft bread to the package of brown sugar, close the bag tightly, and in a few hours the sugar will be soft again. If you need it in a hurry, simply grate the amount called for with a hand grater. Or, put brown sugar and a cup of water (do not add to the sugar, set it alongside of it) in a covered pan. Place in the oven (low heat) for a while. Or, buy liquid brown sugar.

Thawing frozen meat
54. Seal the meat in a plastic bag and place in a bowl of very warm water. Or, put in a bag and let cold water run over it for an hour or so.

Caked or clogged salt
55. Tightly wrap a piece of aluminum foil around the salt shaker. This will keep the dampness out of the salt. To prevent clogging, keep 5 to 10 grains of rice inside your shaker.

Soggy potato chips, cereal and crackers
56. If potato chips lose their freshness, place under the broiler for a few moments. Care must be taken not to brown them. You can crisp soggy cereal and crackers by putting them on a cookie sheet and heating for a few minutes in the oven.

Pancake syrup
57. To make an inexpensive syrup for pancakes, save small amounts of leftover jams and jellies in a jar. Or, fruit-flavored syrup can be made by adding 2 cups sugar to 1 cup of any kind of fruit juice and cooking until it boils.

Easy topping
58. A good topping for gingerbread, coffeecake, etc., can easily be made by freezing the syrup from canned fruit and adding 1 tablespoon of butter and 1 tablespoon of lemon juice to 2 cups of syrup. Heat until bubbly, and thicken with 2 tablespoons of flour.

Tasty cheese sandwiches
59. Toast cheese sandwiches in a frying pan lightly greased with ba-

con fat for a delightful new flavor.

No spattering or sticking
60. To keep frying food from spattering, invert a metal colander over the pan, allowing steam to escape.
61. Always heat the frying pan before adding oil or butter. This will keep things from sticking to the pan.
62. Boil vinegar in a brand new frying pan to keep things from sticking to it.

Hurry-up hamburgers
63. Poke a hole in the middle of the patties while shaping them. The burgers will cook faster and the holes will disappear when done.

Shrinkless links
64. Boil sausage links for about 8 minutes before frying and they will shrink less and not break at all. Or, you can roll them lightly in flour before frying.

Frozen bread
65. Put frozen bread loaves in a clean brown paper bag and place for 5 minutes in a 325° oven to thaw completely.

Removing the corn silk
66. Dampen a paper towel or terry cloth and brush downward on the cob of corn. Every strand should come off.

Nuts
67. To quickly crack a large amount of nuts, put in a bag and gently hammer until they are cracked open. Then remove nutmeats with a pick.
68. If nuts are stale, place them in the oven at 250° F. and leave them there for 5 or 10 minutes. The heat will revive them.

Preventing boil-overs
69. Add a lump of butter or a few teaspoons of cooking oil to the water. Rice, noodles or spaghetti will not boil over or stick together.

Softening butter
70. Soften butter quickly by grating it. Or heat a small pan and place it upside-down over the butter dish for several minutes. Or place in the microwave for a few seconds.

Measuring sticky liquids
71. Before measuring honey or syrup, oil the cup with cooking oil and rinse in hot water.

Scalded milk
72. Add a bit of sugar (without stirring) to milk to prevent it from scorching.
73. Rinse the pan with cold water before scalding milk, and it will be much easier to clean.

Tenderizing meat
74. Boiled meat: Add a tablespoon of vinegar to the cooking water.
75. Tough meat or game: Make a marinade of equal parts cooking vinegar and heated bouillon. Marinate for 2 hours.
76. Steak: Simply rub in a mixture of cooking vinegar and oil. Allow to stand for 2 hours.
77. Chicken: To stew an old hen, soak it in vinegar for several hours before cooking. It will taste like a spring chicken.

Instant white sauce
78. Blend together 1 cup soft butter and 1 cup flour. Spread in an ice cube tray, chill well, cut into 16 cubes before storing in a plastic bag in the freezer. For medium-thick sauce, drop 1 cube into 1 cup of milk and heat slowly, stirring as it thickens.

Unpleasant cooking odors
79. While cooking vegetables that give off unpleasant odors, simmer a small pan of vinegar on top of the stove. Or, add vinegar to the cooking water. To remove the odor of fish from cooking and serving implements, rinse in vinegar water.

Don't lose those vitamins
80. *Put vegetables in water after the water boils - not before - to be sure to preserve all the vegetables' vitamins.*

Clean and deodorize your cutting board
81. *Bleach it clean with lemon juice. Take away strong odors like onion with baking soda. Just rub it in.*

Keep the color in beets
82. *If you find that your beets tend to lose color when you boil them, add a little lemon juice.*

No-smell cabbage
83. *Two things to do to keep cabbage smell from filling the kitchen: don't overcook it (keep it crisp) and put half a lemon in the water when you boil it.*

A great energy saver
84. *When you're near the end of the baking time, turn the oven off and keep the door closed. The heat will stay the same long enough to finish baking your cake or pie and you'll save all that energy.*

Grating cheese
85. *Chill the cheese before grating and it will take much less time.*

Special looking pies
86. *Give a unique look to your pies by using pinking shears to cut the dough. Make a pinked lattice crust!*

Removing ham rind
87. *Before placing ham in the roasting pan, slit rind lengthwise on the underside. The rind will peel away as the ham cooks, and can be easily removed.*

Sluggish catsup
88. *Push a drinking straw to the bottom of the bottle and remove. This admits enough air to start the catsup flowing.*

Unmolding gelatin
89. *Rinse the mold pan in cold water and coat with salad oil. The oil will give the gelatin a nice luster and it will easily fall out of the mold.*

Leftover squash
90. *Squash that is left over can be improved by adding some maple syrup before reheated.*

No-spill cupcakes
91. *An ice cream scoop can be used to fill cupcake papers without spilling.*

Slicing cake or torte
92. *Use dental floss to slice evenly and cleanly through a cake or torte - simply stretch a length of the floss taut and press down through the cake.*

Ice cream
93. *Buy bulk quantities of ice cream and pack in small margarine containers. These provide individual servings.*

Canning peaches
94. *Don't bother to remove skins when canning or freezing peaches. They will taste better and be more nutritious with the skin on.*

Angel food cookies
95. *Stale angel food cake can be cut into 1/2" slices and shaped with cookie cutters to make delicious "cookies". Just toast in the oven for a few minutes.*

How to chop garlic
96. *Chop in a small amount of salt to prevent pieces from sticking to the knife or chopped board. Then pulverize with the tip of the knife.*

Excess fat on soups or stews
97. *Remove fat from stews or soups by refrigerating and eliminating fat as it rises and hardens on the surface. Or add lettuce leaves to the pot - the fat will cling to them. Discard lettuce before serving.*

Broiled meat drippings
98. *Place a piece of bread under the rack on which you are broiling meat. Not only will this absorb the dripping fat, but it will reduce the chance of the fat catching on fire.*

Fake sour cream
99. *To cut down on calories, run cottage cheese through the blender. It can be flavored with chives, extracts, etc., and used in place of mayonnaise.*

Browned butter
100. *Browning brings out the flavor of the butter, so only half as much is needed for seasoning vegetables if it is browned before it is added.*

Cooking dried beans
101. *When cooking dried beans, add salt after cooking; if salt is added at the start, it will slow the cooking process.*

Tasty carrots
102. *Adding sugar and horseradish to cooked carrots improves their flavor.*

Carrot marinade
103. *Marinate carrot sticks in dill pickle juice.*

Clean cukes
104. *A ball of nylon net cleans and smooths cucumbers when making pickles.*

Fresh garlic
105. *Peel garlic and store in a covered jar of vegetable oil. The garlic will stay fresh and the oil will be nicely flavored for salad dressings.*

Leftover waffles
106. *Freeze waffles that are left; they can be reheated in the toaster.*

Fluffy rice
107. *Rice will be fluffier and whiter if you add 1 teaspoon of lemon juice to each quart of water.*

Nutritious rice
108. *Cook rice in liquid saved from cooking vegetables to add flavor and nutrition. A nutty taste can be achieved by adding wheat germ to the rice.*

Perfect noodles
109. *When cooking noodles, bring required amount of water to a boil, add noodles, turn heat off and allow to stand for 20 minutes. This prevents overboiling and the chore of stirring. Noodles won't stick to the pan with this method.*

Easy croutons
110. *Make delicious croutons for soup or salad by saving toast, cutting into cubes, and sauteing in garlic butter.*

Baked fish
111. *To keep fish from sticking to the pan, bake on a bed of chopped onion, celery and parsley. This also adds a nice flavor to the fish.*

Non-sticking bacon
112. *Roll a package of bacon into a tube before opening. This will loosen the slices and keep them from sticking together.*

Tasty hot dogs
113. *Boil hot dogs in sweet pickle juice and a little water for a different taste.*

Golden-brown chicken
114. *For golden-brown fried chicken, roll it in powdered milk instead of flour.*

Doubler boiler hint
115. *Toss a few marbles in the bottom of a double boiler. When the water boils down, the noise will let you know!*

Flour puff
116. *Keep a powder puff in your flour container to easily dust your rolling pin or pastry board.*

Jar labels
117. *Attach canning labels to the lids instead of the sides of jelly jars, to prevent the chore of removing the labels when the contents are gone.*

Different meatballs
118. *Try using crushed cornflakes or corn bread instead of bread crumbs in a meatball recipe. Or use onion-flavored potato chips.*

* * * * * *

CLEAN-UP TIPS

Appliances
119. *To rid yellowing from white appliances try this: Mix together: ½ cup bleach, ¼ cup baking soda and 4 cups warm water. Apply with a sponge and let set for 10 minutes. Rinse and dry thoroughly.*
120. *Instead of using commercial waxes, shine with rubbing alcohol.*
121. *For quick clean-ups, rub with equal parts of water and household ammonia.*
122. *Or, try club soda. It cleans and polishes at the same time.*

Blender
123. *Fill part way with hot water and add a drop of detergent. Cover and turn it on for a few seconds. Rinse and drain dry.*

Breadboards
124. *To rid cutting board of onion, garlic or fish smell, cut a lime or lemon in 2 and rub the surface with the cut side of the fruit.*
125. *Or, make a paste of baking soda and water and apply generously. Rinse.*

Copper pots
126. *Fill a spray bottle with vinegar and add 3 tablespoons of salt. Spray solution liberally on copper pot. Let set for a while, then simply rub clean.*
127. *Dip lemon halves in salt and rub.*
128. *Or, rub with Worcestershire*

sauce or catsup. The tarnish will disappear.
129. *Clean with toothpaste and rinse.*

Burnt and scorched pans
130. *Sprinkle burnt pans liberally with baking soda, adding just enough water to moisten. Let stand for several hours. You can generally lift the burned portions right out of the pan.*
131. *Stubborn stains on non-stick cookware can be removed by boiling 2 tablespoons of baking soda, ½ cup vinegar and 1 cup water for 10 minutes. Re-season pan with salad oil.*

Cast-iron skillets
132. *Clean the outside of the pan with commercial oven cleaner. Let set for 2 hours and the accumulated black stains can be removed with vinegar and water.*

Can opener
133. *Loosen grime by brushing with an old toothbrush. To thoroughly clean blades, run a paper towel through the cutting process.*

Enamelware or casserole dishes
134. *Fill a dish that contains stuck food bits with boiling water and 2 tablespoons of baking soda. Let it stand and wash out.*

Dishes
135. *Save time and money by using the cheapest brand of dishwashing detergent available, but add a few tablespoons of vinegar to the dishwater. The vinegar will cut the grease and leave your dishes sparkling clean.*
136. *Before washing fine china and crystal, place a towel on the bottom of the sink to act as a cushion.*
137. *To remove coffee or tea stains and cigarette burns from fine china, rub with a damp cloth dipped in baking soda.*

Dishwasher
138. *Run a cup of white vinegar*

through the entire cycle in an empty dishwasher to remove all soap film.

Clogged drains

139. When a drain is clogged with grease, pour a cup of salt and a cup of baking soda into the drain followed by a kettle of boiling water. The grease will usually dissolve immediately and open the drain.
140. Coffee grounds are a no-no. They do a nice job of clogging, especially if they get mixed with grease.

Garbage disposal

141. Grind a half lemon or orange rind in the disposal to remove any unpleasant odor.

Glassware

142. Never put a delicate glass in hot water bottom side first; it will crack from sudden expansion. The most delicate glassware will be safe if it is slipped in edgewise.
143. Vinegar is a must when washing crystal. Rinse in 1 part vinegar to 3 parts warm water. Air dry.
144. When one glass is tucked inside another, do not force them apart. Fill the top glass with cold water and dip the lower one in hot water. They will come apart without breaking.

Grater

145. For a fast and simple clean-up, rub salad oil on the grater before using.
146. Use a toothbrush to brush lemon rind, cheese, onion or whatever out of the grater before washing it.

Meat grinder

147. Before washing, run a piece of bread through it.

Oven

148. Following a spill, sprinkle with salt immediately. When oven is cool, brush off burnt food and wipe with a damp sponge.
149. Sprinkle bottom of oven with automatic dishwasher soap and cover with wet paper towels. Let stand for a few hours.
150. A quick way to clean oven parts is to place a bath towel in the bathtub and pile all removable parts from the oven onto it. Draw enough hot water to just cover the parts and sprinkle a cup of dishwasher soap over it. While you are cleaning the inside of the oven, the rest will be cleaning itself.
151. An inexpensive oven cleaner: Set oven on warm for about 20 minutes, then turn off. Place a small dish of full strength ammonia on the top shelf. Put a large pan of boiling water on the bottom shelf and let it set overnight. In the morning, open oven and let it air a while before washing off with soap and water. Even the hard baked-on grease will wash off easily.

Plastic cups, dishes and containers

152. Coffee or tea stains can be scoured with baking soda.
153. Or, fill the stained cup with hot water and drop in a few denture cleanser tablets. Let soak for 1 hour.
154. To rid foul odors from plastic containers, place crumpled-up newspaper (black and white only) into the container. Cover tightly and leave overnight.

Refrigerator

155. To help eliminate odors fill a small bowl with charcoal (the kind used for potted plants) and place it on a shelf in the refrigerator. It absorbs odors rapidly.
156. An open box of baking soda will absorb food odors for at least a month or two.
157. A little vanilla poured on a piece of cotton and placed in the refrigerator will eliminate odors.
158. To prevent mildew from forming, wipe with vinegar. The acid effectively kills the mildew fungus.
159. Use a glycerine-soaked cloth to wipe sides and shelves. Future spills wipe up easily. And after the freezer has been defrosted, coat

the inside coils with glycerine. The next time you defrost, the ice will loosen quickly and drop off in sheets.

160. Wash inside and out with a mixture of 3 tablespoons of baking soda in a quart of warm water.

Sinks

161. For a sparkling white sink, place paper towels across the bottom of your sink and saturate with household bleach. Let set for ½ hour or so.

162. Rub stainless steel sinks with lighter fluid if rust marks appear. After the rust disappears, wipe with your regular kitchen cleanser.

163. Use a cloth dampened with rubbing alcohol to remove water spots from stainless steel.

164. Spots on stainless steel can also be removed with white vinegar.

165. Club soda will shine up stainless steel sinks in a jiffy.

Sponges

166. Wash in your dishwasher or soak overnight in salt water or baking soda added to water.

Teakettle

167. To remove lime deposits, fill with equal parts of vinegar and water. Bring to a boil and allow to stand overnight.

Thermos bottle

168. Fill the bottle with warm water, add 1 teaspoon of baking soda and allow to soak.

Tin pie pans

169. Remove rust by dipping a raw potato in cleaning powder and scouring.

Fingerprints off the kitchen door and walls

170. Take away fingerprints and grime with a solution of half water and half ammonia. Put in a spray bottle from one of these expensive cleaning products, you'll never have to buy them again.

Formica tops

171. Polish them to a sparkle with club soda.

* * * * * *

KEEPING FOODS FRESH AND
FOOD STORAGE

Celery and lettuce

172. Store in refrigerator in paper bags instead of plastic. Leave the outside leaves and stalks on until ready to use.

Onions

173. Wrap individually in foil to keep them from becoming soft or sprouting.

174. Once an onion has been cut in half, rub the leftover side with butter and it will keep fresh longer.

Cheese

175. Wrap cheese in a vinegar-dampened cloth to keep it from drying out.

Milk

176. Milk at room temperature may spoil cold milk, so don't pour back into the carton.

Brown sugar

177. Wrap in a plastic bag and store in refrigerator in a coffee can with a snap-on lid.

Cocoa

178. Store cocoa in a glass jar in a dry and cool place.

Cakes

179. Putting half an apple in the cake box will keep cake moist.

Ice cream

180. Ice cream that has been opened and returned to the freezer sometimes forms a waxlike film on the top. To prevent this, after part of the ice cream has been removed press a piece of waxed paper against the surface and reseal the carton.

Lemons
181. *Store whole lemons in a tightly sealed jar of water in the refrigerator. They will yield much more juice than when first purchased.*

Limes
182. *Store limes, wrapped in tissue paper, on lower shelf of the refrigerator.*

Smoked meats
183. *Wrap ham or bacon in a vinegar-soaked cloth, then in waxed paper to preserve freshness.*

Strawberries
184. *Keep in a colander in the refrigerator. Wash just before serving.*

Soda crackers
185. *Wrap tightly and store in the refrigerator.*

Vegetables with tops
186. *Remove the tops on carrots, beets, etc. before storing.*

Bread
187. *A rib of celery in your bread bag will keep the bread fresh for a longer time.*

Cookies
188. *Place crushed tissue paper on the bottom of your cookie jar.*

Cottage cheese
189. *Store carton upside-down. It will keep twice as long.*

Garlic
190. *Garlic cloves can be kept in the freezer. When ready to use, peel and chop before thawing.*
191. *Or, garlic cloves will never dry out if you store them in a bottle of cooking oil. After the garlic is used up, you can use the garlic-flavored oil for salad dressing.*

Honey
192. *Put honey in small plastic freezer containers to prevent sugaring. It also thaws out in a short time.*

Marshmallows
193. *They will not dry out if stored in the freezer. Simply cut with scissors when ready to use.*

Olive oil
194. *You can lengthen the life of olive oil by adding a cube of sugar to the bottle.*

Parsley
195. *Keep fresh and crisp by storing in a wide-mouth jar with a tight lid. Parsley may also be frozen.*

Popcorn
196. *It should always be kept in the freezer. Not only will it stay fresh, but freezing helps eliminate "old-maids".*

* * * * * *

SUBSTITUTES
For bread crumbs
197. *Use crushed corn or wheat flakes, or other dry cereal. Or use potato flakes.*

For butter
198. *Use ⅞ cup of solid shortening plus ½ teaspoon of salt.*

For fresh milk
199. *To substitute 1 cup of fresh milk, use ½ cup each of evaporated milk and water.*
200. *For 1 cup of whole milk, prepare 1 liquid cup of nonfat dry milk and 2½ teaspoons butter or margarine.*

For sugar
201. *Use brown sugar, although it will result in a slight molasses flavor.*

For superfine sugar
202. *Process regular granulated sugar in your blender.*

For red and green sweet pepper
203. *Use canned pimientos.*

For vanilla extract
204. *Use grated lemon or orange rind for flavoring instead. Or try a little cinnamon or nutmeg.*

For flour
205. *Use 1 tablespoon cornstarch instead of 2 tablespoons of flour. Or try using instant potatoes or cornmeal.*

For buttermilk
206. *Use 1 tablespoon of lemon juice or vinegar and enough fresh milk to make 1 cup. Let it stand 5 minutes before using.*

For catsup
207. *Use a cup of tomato sauce added to 1¼ cups of brown sugar, 2 tablespoons of vinegar, ¼ teaspoon of cinnamon and a dash of ground cloves and allspice.*

For unsweetened chocolate
208. *Use 1 tablespoon of shortening plus 3 tablespoons of unsweetened cocoa to equal 1 square of unsweetened chocolate.*

For corn syrup
209. *Use ¼ cup of water or other type of liquid called for in the recipe, plus 1 cup of sugar.*

For eggs
210. *Add 3 or 4 extra tablespoons of liquid called for in the recipe. Or, when you're 1 egg shy for a recipe that calls for many, substitute 1 teaspoon of cornstarch.*

For cake flour
211. *Use ⅞ cup of all-purpose flour for each cup of cake flour called for in a recipe.*

For fresh herbs and spices
212. *For ⅓ the amount of dried herbs or spices. Dried herbs are more concentrated.*

For honey
213. *To substitute 1 cup of honey, use 1¼ cups of sugar and ¼ cup of water or other liquid called for in the recipe.*

*   *   *   *   *   *

II. TO REMOVE STAINS FROM WASHABLES

Alcoholic beverages
214. *Pre-soak or sponge fresh stains immediately with cold water, then with cold water and glycerine. Rinse with vinegar for a few seconds if stain remains. These stains may turn brown with age. If wine stain remains, rub with concentrated detergent; wait 15 minutes; rinse. Repeat if necessary. Wash with detergent in hottest water safe for fabric.*

Blood
215. *Pre-soak in cold or warm water at least 30 minutes. If stain remains, soak in lukewarm ammonia water (3 tablespoons per gallon water). Rinse. If stain remains, work in detergent, and wash, using bleach safe for fabric.*

Candle wax
216. *Use a dull knife to scrape off as much as possible. Place fabric between 2 blotters or facial tissues and press with warm iron. Remove color stain with non-flammable dry cleaning solvent. Wash with detergent in the hottest water safe for fabric.*

Chewing gum
217. *Rub area with ice, then scrape off with a dull blade. Sponge with dry cleaning solvent; allow to air dry. Wash in detergent and hottest water safe for fabric.*

Chocolate and cocoa
218. *Pre-soak stain in cold or warm water. Wash in hot water with detergent. Remove any grease stains with dry cleaning solvent. If color remains, sponge with hydrogen*

peroxide, wash again.

Coffee
219. *Sponge or soak with cold water as soon as possible. Wash, using detergent and bleach safe for fabric. Remove cream grease stains with non-flammable dry cleaning solvent. Wash again.*

Crayon
220. *Scrape with dull blade. Wash in hottest water safe for fabric, with detergent and 1 to 2 cups of baking soda. NOTE: If full load is crayon stained, take to cleaners or coin-op dry cleaning machines.*

Deodorants
221. *Sponge area with white vinegar. If stain remains, soak with denatured alcohol. Wash with detergent in hottest water safe for fabric.*

Dye
222. *If dye transfers from a non-colorfast item during washing, immediately bleach discolored items. Repeat as necessary BEFORE drying. On whites use color remover. CAUTION: Do not use color remover in washer, or around washer and dryer as it may damage the finish.*

Egg
223. *Scrape with dull blade. Presoak in cold or warm water for at least 30 minutes. Remove grease with dry cleaning solvent. Wash in hottest water safe for fabric, with detergent.*

Fruit and fruit juices
224. *Sponge with cold water. Presoak in cold or warm water for at least 30 minutes. Wash with detergent and bleach safe for fabric.*

Grass
225. *Pre-soak in cold water for at least 30 minutes. Rinse. Pre-treat with detergent, hot water, and bleach safe for fabric. On acetate and colored fabrics, use 1 part of alcohol to 2 parts water.*

Grease, oil, tar
226. *Method 1: Use powder or chalk absorbents to remove as much grease as possible. Pre-treat with detergent or non-flammable dry cleaning solvent, or liquid shampoo. Wash in hottest water safe for fabric, using plenty of detergent.*
227. *Method 2: Rub spot with lard and sponge with a non-flammable dry cleaning solvent. Wash in hottest water and detergent safe for fabric.*

Ink-ball-point pen
228. *Pour denatured alcohol through stain. Rub in petroleum jelly. Sponge with non-flammable dry cleaning solvent. Soak in detergent solution. Wash with detergent and bleach safe for fabric.*

Lipstick
229. *Loosen stain with a non-flammable dry cleaning solvent. Rub detergent in until stain outline is gone. Wash in hottest water and detergent safe for fabric.*

Meat juices
230. *Scrape with dull blade. Presoak in cold or warm water for 30 minutes. Wash with detergent and bleach safe for fabric.*

Mildew
231. *Pre-treat as soon as possible with detergent. Wash. If any stain remains, sponge with lemon juice and salt. Dry in sun. Wash, using hottest water, detergent and bleach safe for fabric. NOTE: Mildew is very hard to remove; treat promptly.*

Milk, cream, ice cream
232. *Pre-soak in cold or warm water for 30 minutes. Wash. Sponge any grease spots with non-flammable dry cleaning solvent. Wash again.*

Nail polish
233. *Sponge with polish remover or banana oil. Wash. If stain remains, sponge with denatured alcohol to*

which a few drops of ammonia have been added. Wash again. Do not use polish remover on acetate or triacetate fabrics.

Paint
234. Oil base: Sponge stains with turpentine, cleaning fluid or paint remover. Pre-treat and wash in hot water. For old stains, sponge with banana oil and then with non-flammable dry cleaning solvent. Wash again.
235. Water base: Scrape off paint with dull blade. Wash with detergent in water as hot as is safe for fabric.

Perspiration
236. Sponge fresh stain with ammonia; old stain with vinegar. Pre-soak in cold or warm water. Rinse. Wash in hottest water safe for fabric. If fabric is yellowed, use bleach. If stain still remains, dampen and sprinkle with meat tenderizer, or pepsin. Let stand 1 hour. Brush off and wash. For persistent odor, sponge with colorless mouthwash.

Rust
237. Soak in lemon juice and salt or axolic acid solution (3 tablespoons oxalic acid to 1 pint warm water). A commercial rust remover may be used. CAUTION: HANDLE POISONOUS RUST REMOVERS CAREFULLY. KEEP OUT OF REACH OF CHILDREN. NEVER USE OXALIC ACID OR ANY RUST REMOVER AROUND WASHER OR DRYER AS IT CAN DAMAGE THE FINISH. SUCH CHEMICALS MAY ALSO REMOVE PERMANENT PRESS FABRIC FINISHES.

Scorch
238. Wash with detergent and bleach safe for fabric. On heavier scorching, cover stain with cloth dampened with hydrogen peroxide. Cover this with dry cloth and press with hot iron. Rinse well. CAUTION: Severe scorching cannot be removed because of fabric damage.

Soft drinks
239. Sponge immediately with cold water and alcohol. Heat and detergent may set stain.

Tea
240. Sponge or soak with cold water as soon as possible. Wash using detergent and bleach safe for fabric.

* * * * * *

III. CARPETS AND FLOORS

Flattened shag carpets
241. Raise flattened spots in your carpet where heavy furniture has stood by using a steam iron. Hold the iron over the spot and build up a good steam. Then brush up the carpet.

Candle drippings
242. For spilled wax on carpet, use a brown paper bag as a blotter and run a hot iron over it, which will absorb the wax.

Dog stains
243. Blot up excess moisture with paper towel. Pour club soda on the spot and continue blotting. Lay a towel over the spot and set a heavy object on top in order to absorb all the moisture.

Rug care
244. When washing and drying foam-backed throw rugs, never wash in hot water, and use the "air only" dryer setting to dry. Heat will ruin foam.

Cleaning rugs
245. If the rug is only slightly dirty, you can clean it with cornmeal. Use a stiff brush to work the cornmeal into the pile of the rug. Take it all out with the vacuum.

What to do with new carpet
246. Wait about 3 months before attempting to clean your new carpet. It needs that amount of time to

spring up and keep its normal nap.

Spills on the rug
247. When spills happen, go to the bathroom and grab a can of shaving cream. Squirt it on the spot then rinse off with water.

Liven up your carpet
248. Give your carpet a new lease on life. Sprinkle some salt on it right before you vacuum. The rug will be much brighter when you have finished vacuuming.

Ballpoint ink marks
249. Saturate the spots with hairspray. Allow to dry. Brush lightly with a solution of water and vinegar.

Glue
250. Glue can be loosened by saturating the spot with a cloth soaked in vinegar.

Repairing braided rugs
251. Braided rugs often rip apart. Instead of sewing them, use clear fabric glue to repair. It's that fast and easy.

Repairing a burn
252. Remove some fuzz from the carpet, either by shaving or pulling out with a tweezer. Roll into the shape of the burn. Apply a good cement glue to the backing of the rug and press the fuzz down into the burned spot. Cover with a piece of cleansing tissue and place a heavy book on top. This will cause the glue to dry very slowly and will get the best results.

Spot remover for outdoor carpeting
253. Spray spots liberally with a prewash commercial spray. Let it set several minutes, then hose down and watch the spots disappear.

Blood on the rug
254. When you get blood on your rug, rub off as much as you can at first, then take a cloth soaked in cold water and wet the spot, wiping it up as you go. If a little bit remains, pour some ammonia onto the cool, wet cloth and lightly wipe that over the spot, too. Rinse it right away with cold water.

Crayon Marks
255. Use silver polish to remove from vinyl tile or linoleum.

Spilled nail polish
256. Allow to almost dry, then peel off of waxed floors or tile.

Tar spots
257. Use paste wax to remove tar from floors. Works on shoes, too.

Dusting floors
258. Stretch a nylon stocking over the dust mop. After using, discard the stocking and you will have a clean mop.

Varnished floors
259. Use cold tea to clean woodwork and varnished floors.

Spilled grease
260. Rub floor with ice cubes to solidify grease. Scrape up excess and wash with soapy water.

Quick shine
261. Put a piece of waxed paper under your dust mop. Dirt will stick to the mop and the wax will shine your floors.

Unmarred floors
262. Put thick old socks over the legs of heavy furniture when moving across floors.

Wood floor care
263. Never use water or water-based cleaners on wood floors. Over a period of time, warping and swelling will develop.

Floor polisher
264. When cleaning the felt pads of your floor polisher, place the pads between layers of newspaper and

press with an iron to absorb built-up wax.

Garage floors
265. In an area where a large amount of oil has spilled, lay several thicknesses of newspaper. Saturate the paper with water; press flat against the floor. When dry, remove the newspaper and the spots will have disappeared.

Basement floors
266. Sprinkle sand on oily spots, let it absorb the oil, and sweep up.

Fix those loose linoleum edges
267. Take a knife with some tile adhesive and work it under the loose part. Put a heavy weight, such as a big stack of books, over the whole area and keep it weighed down for the amount of time it says on the can of adhesive.

Stop squeaking floors
268. Just dust some talcum powder between the cracks and it should do the job. If you have really serious squeaking, it could be that you need to wedge in some slivers of wood to the underneath side.

Heel marks
269. Just take a pencil eraser and wipe them off.

. . . . . .

IV. WINDOWS

Window cleaning
270. Newspaper is much cheaper to use for drying freshly-washed windows than paper toweling.

Drying windows
271. Dry the inside panes with up-and-down strokes, and the outside with back-and-forth motions to see which side has smudges.

Window cleaning solution
272. The best mixture for cleaning windows is ½ cup of ammonia, 1 cup of white vinegar and 2 table-spoons of cornstarch in a bucket of warm water.

Cold weather window cleaning
273. Add ½ cup of rubbing alcohol to the above mixture on cold days to prevent ice from forming on your windows.

Clean window sills
274. To remove spots on window sills, rub the surface with rubbing alcohol.

Puttying windows
275. Mix some putty to match the woodwork before puttying windows.

Loosening window panes
276. Dig through old putty with a very hot instrument to loosen a window pane.

Aluminum window frames
277. Use cream silver polish to clean aluminum window frames.

Grease spots
278. Any cola drink will remove grease spots from windows.

Numbered windows
279. When cleaning, painting or changing windows, number each with a ballpoint pen and put the corresponding number inside the proper window frame.

Window shade tears
280. Repair with colorless nail polish. This works wonders on small tears.

Cleaning screens
281. For a thorough job, brush on both sides with kerosene. Wipe with a clean cloth. This method will also prevent rust from forming. Be sure to dust the screens with a small paintbrush before you begin.
282. For small jobs, rub a brush-type hair roller lightly over the screen and see how easily it picks up all the lint and dust.

* * * * * *

V. FURNITURE

Fantastic polish
283. Use ⅓ cup each boiled linseed oil, turpentine and vinegar. Mix together and shake well. Apply with a soft cloth and wipe completely dry. Wipe again with another soft cloth. Do not try to boil your own linseed oil - it is not the same. Buy it at a hardware or paint store.

To remove polish build-up
284. Mix ½ cup vinegar and ½ cup water. Rub with a soft cloth that has been moistened with solution, but wrung out. Dry immediately with another soft cloth.

Polishing carved furniture
285. Dip an old soft toothbrush into furniture polish and brush lightly.

Cigarette burns
286. For small minor burns, try rubbing mayonnaise into the burn. Let set for a while before wiping off with a soft cloth.
287. Burns can be repaired with a wax stick (available in all colors at paint and hardware stores). Gently scrape away the charred finish. Heat a knife blade and melt the shellac stick against the heated blade. Smooth over damaged area with your finger. But always consider the value of the furniture. It might be better to have a professional make the repair.
288. Or, make a paste of rottenstone (available at hardware stores) and salad oil. Rub into the burned spot only, following the grain of wood. Wipe clean with a cloth that has been dampened in oil. Wipe dry and apply your favorite furniture polish.

Scratches
289. Make sure you always rub with the grain of the wood when repairing a scratch. Walnut: Remove the meat from a fresh, unsalted walnut or pecan nut. Break it in half and rub the scratch with the broken side of the nut.
290. Mahogany: You can either rub the scratch with a dark brown crayon or buff with brown paste wax.
291. Red Mahogany: Apply ordinary iodine with a number 0 artist's brush.
292. Maple: Combine equal amounts of iodine and denatured alcohol. Apply with a Q-tip, then dry, wax and buff.
293. Ebony: Use black shoe polish, black eyebrow pencil or black crayon.
294. Teakwood: Rub very gently with 0000 steel wool. Rub in equal amounts of linseed oil and turpentine.
295. Light-finished furniture: Scratches can be hidden by using tan shoe polish. However, only on shiny finishes.
296. For all minor scratches: Cover each scratch with a generous amount of white petroleum jelly. Allow it to remain on for 24 hours. Rub into wood. Remove excess and polish as usual.
297. For larger scratches: Fill by rubbing with a wax stick (available in all colors at your hardware or paint store) or a crayon that matches the finish of the wood.

Removing paper that is stuck to a wood surface
298. Do not scrape with a knife. Pour any salad oil, a few drops at a time, on the paper. Let set for a while and rub with a soft cloth. Repeat the procedure until the paper is completely gone.
299. Old decals can be removed easily by painting them with several coats of white vinegar. Give the vinegar time to soak in, then gently scrape off.

Three solutions to remove white water rings and spots
300. Dampen a soft cloth with wa-

ter and put a dab of toothpaste on it. For stubborn stains, add baking soda to the toothpaste.

301. Make a paste of butter or mayonnaise and cigarette ashes. Apply to spot and buff away.

302. Apply a paste of salad oil and salt. Let stand briefly. Wipe and polish.

Marble table-top stains

303. Sprinkle salt on a fresh-cut lemon. Rub very lightly over stain. Do not rub hard or you will ruin the polished surface. Wash off with soap and water.

304. Scour with a water and baking soda paste. Let stand for a few minutes before rinsing with warm water.

Removing candle wax from wooden finishes

305. Soften the wax with a hair dryer. Remove wax with paper toweling and wash down with a solution of vinegar and water.

Plastic table tops

306. You will find that a coat of Turtle Wax is a quick pick-up for dulled plastic table tops and counters.

307. Or, rub in toothpaste and buff.

Glass table tops

308. Rub in a little lemon juice. Dry with paper towels and shine with newspaper for a sparkling table.

309. Toothpaste will remove small scratches from glass.

Chrome cleaning

310. For sparkling clean chrome without streaks, use a cloth dampened in ammonia.

Removing glue

311. Cement glue can be removed by rubbing with cold cream, peanut butter or salad oil.

Wicker

312. Wicker needs moisture, so use a humidifier in the winter.

313. To prevent drying out, apply lemon oil occasionally.

314. Never let wicker freeze. This will cause cracking and splitting.

315. Wash with a solution of warm salt water to keep from turning yellow.

Metal furniture

316. To remove rust, a good scrubbing with turpentine should accomplish this job.

Vinyl upholstery

317. Never oil vinyl as this will make it hard. It is almost impossible to soften again. For proper cleaning, sprinkle baking soda or vinegar on a rough, damp cloth, then wash with a mild dishwashing soap.

Leather upholstery

318. Prevent leather from cracking by polishing regularly with a cream made of 1 part vinegar and 2 parts linseed oil. Clean with a damp cloth and saddle soap.

Grease stains

319. Absorb grease on furniture by pouring salt on the spill immediately.

Soiled upholstery

320. Rub soiled cotton upholstery fabric with an artgum eraser or squares (purchased at stationery store).

* * * * * *

VI. LAUNDRY

Spot removal

321. Two parts water and one part rubbing alcohol are the basic ingredients in any commercial spot remover.

Clean machine

322. Fill your washer with warm water and add a gallon of distilled vinegar. Run the machine through the entire cycle to unclog and clean soap scum from hoses.

Too sudsy
323. When your washer overflows with too many suds, sprinkle salt in the water - the suds will disappear.

Final rinse
324. Add a cup of white vinegar to the final rinse when washing clothes to make sure the alkalines in the soap are dissolved.

Hand-washed sweaters
325. Add a capful of hair cream rinse to the final rinse water when washing sweaters.

Whiter fabric
326. Linen or cotton can be whitened by boiling in a mixture of 1 part cream of tartar and 3 parts water.

Whitest socks
327. Boil socks in water to which a lemon slice has been added.

Clean work clothes
328. To your wash water, add ½ cup of household ammonia.

Freshen feather pillows
329. Put feather pillows in the dryer and tumble, then air outside.

Lintless corduroy
330. While corduroy is still damp, brush with clothes brush to remove all lint.

Ironing tip
331. When pressing pants, iron the top part on the wrong side. Iron the legs on the right side. This gives the pockets and waistband a smooth look.

Creaseless garments
332. Take an empty cardboard paper towel roll and cut through it lengthwise. Slip it over a wire hanger to prevent a crease from forming in the garment to be hung on the hanger.

Remove creases from hems
333. Sponge material with a white vinegar solution and press flat to remove creases in hems.

Bedroom ironing
334. A good place to iron is in the bedroom. Closets are nearby to hang clothes up immediately, and the bed makes a good surface on which to fold clothes and separate items into piles.

Ironing board cover
335. When washing your ironing board cover, attach it to the board while it is still damp. When it dries, the surface will be completely smooth.
336. Starch your ironing board cover. This helps the cover stay clean longer.

Lint remover
337. Add a yard of nylon netting to your dryer with the wet clothes - it will catch most of the lint.

Washer advice
338. Button all buttons on clothing and turn inside out before putting into the washer. Fewer buttons will fall off and garments will fade less if turned inside out.

Soiled collars
339. Use a small paintbrush and brush hair shampoo into soiled shirt collars before laundering. Shampoo is made to dissolve body oils.

Faster ironing
340. Place a strip of heavy-duty aluminum foil over the entire length of the ironing board and cover with pad. As you iron, heat will reflect through to the underside of the garment.

Ironing embroidery
341. Lay the embroidery piece upside-down on a Turkish towel before ironing. All the little spaces between the embroidery will be smooth when you are finished.

* * * * * *

VII. BATHROOM

Bathroom tile
342. *Rub ordinary car wax into your ceramic bathroom tiling to clean and refinish. Let it stand 10 minutes and buff or polish.*
343. *Use a typewriter eraser to clean spaces between bathroom tiles.*

Metal shower head
344. *To clean mineral deposits from a clogged shower head, boil it with half a cup of white vinegar.*

Plastic shower head
345. *Soak a plastic shower head in a hot vinegar and water mixture to unclog it.*

Shower curtains
346. *Before hanging shower curtains, soak them in a salt water solution to prevent mildew.*
347. *To remove mildew on shower curtains, wash them in hot soapy water, rub with lemon juice, and let them dry in the sun.*

Bathroom fixtures
348. *Dip a cloth in kerosene or rubbing alcohol to remove scum from your bathroom fixtures.*

Removing film and scum
349. *Use a piece of very fine steel wool to remove film from the shower stall.*

Porcelain cleaners
350. *Lighter fluid will remove most dark, stubborn stains from sink and bathtub.*

Yellowed bathtub
351. *Restore whiteness to a yellowed bathtub by rubbing with a salt and turpentine solution.*

Shower mat tip
352. *Dip a stiff brush in a kerosene and warm water solution to clean the bath mat.*

Rust stains
353. *Spread a paste of hydrogen peroxide and cream of tartar over the area, and add a few drops of ammonia. Let it stand for 2 or 3 hours.*

Rusty tile
354. *Rust stains on tile can be removed with kerosene.*

Cleaning shower doors
355. *Rub glass shower doors with a white vinegar-dampened sponge to remove soap residue.*

Steam-free mirror
356. *If your medicine cabinet has two sliding mirrors, slide one side open before taking a bath or shower. After the bath, you'll have one clean mirror instead of two that are steamed and foggy.*

Steamy bathrooms
357. *If you run about an inch of cold water before adding hot water to your bath, there will be absolutely no steam in your bathroom.*

Medicine cabinet
358. *It's a good idea to go through your medicine cabinet several times a year and throw away medicines that are old or outdated. They could be dangerous.*

Easy bathroom cleaning
359. *Clean your bathroom after a steamy bath or shower. The walls, fixtures, etc., will be much easier to clean because the steam will have loosened the dirt.*

Sink cleaners
360. *Light stains can often be removed by simply rubbing with a cut lemon.*
361. *For dark stains, and especially rust, rub with a paste of borax and lemon juice.*

Dripping faucet
362. If the drip occurs during the night and you can't sleep, simply wrap a cloth around the opening of the faucet.

Sweet-smelling bathroom
363. Place a fabric softener sheet in the wastepaper basket. Or, add a touch of fragrance by dabbing your favorite perfume on a light bulb. When the light is on, the heat releases the aroma.

* * * * * *

VIII. HANDYPERSON

Leaky vase
364. Fix a leaky vase by coating the inside with paraffin and letting it harden.

Plywood cutting
365. Put a strip of masking tape at the point of plywood where you plan to begin sawing to keep it from splitting.

Locating wall studs
366. Move a pocket compass along the wall. When the needle moves, usually the stud will be located at that point. Studs are usually located 16" apart.

Fraying rope
367. Shellac the ends of the rope to prevent fraying.
368. Heat the cut end of nylon cord over a match flame to bond the end together.

Loosening rusty bolts
369. Apply a cloth soaked in any carbonated soda to loosen rusted bolts.

Sandpaper hint
370. By dampening the backing on sandpaper, it will last longer and resist cracking.

Tight screws
371. Loosen a screw by putting a couple of drops of peroxide on it and letting it soak in.

Screwdriver tip
372. Keep a screwdriver tip from slipping by putting chalk on the blade.

Loosening joints
373. Loosen old glue by applying vinegar from an oil can to the joint.

Rule to remember
374. Left is loose and right is tight.

Sticking drawers
375. Rub the runners of drawers with a candle or a bar of soap so they will slide easily.

Stubborn locks
376. Dip key into machine oil or graphite to loosen up a lock.

Loose drawer knobs
377. Before inserting a screw into the knob, coat with fingernail polish to hold it tightly.

Slamming doors
378. Reduce the noise level in your home by putting self-sticking protective pads on the inside edges of cabinet doors, cupboards, etc.

Icy sidewalk tip
379. Sprinkle sand through a strainer on an icy sidewalk to distribute evenly.

Garbage can tip
380. Garbage cans will last longer if they are painted. Use primer on galvanized metal, then paint with matching house paint.

Towel rack tip
381. Replace the bottom screws of towel racks with cup hooks. Small towels and washcloths may be hung from them.

Screen repair
382. Use clear cement glue to repair a small hole in wire screening.

Hairdryer hint
383. *Thaw a frozen pipe with a portable hairdryer.*

Finding a gas leak
384. *Lather the pipes with soapy water. The escaping gas will cause the soapy water to bubble, revealing the damaged areas. You can make a temporary plug by moistening a cake of soap and pressing it over the spot. When the soap hardens, it will effectively close the leak until the gasman comes.*

Hanging pictures
385. *Before you drive nails into the wall, mark the spot with an X of cellophane tape. This trick will keep the plaster from cracking when you start hammering.*
386. *When the landlady says, "no nails in the wall", hang pictures with sewing machine needles. They will hold up to 30 pounds.*

* * * * * *

IX. BEAUTY

Natural facial
387. *A good and inexpensive facial to try: mash half an avocado, spread thickly on face, and remove with warm water 20 minutes later.*

Cuticle treatment
388. *Apply a mixture of equal parts of castor oil and white iodine to your cuticles every night.*

Sunburn relief
389. *A wonderful relief for sunburn pain is the application of mint-flavored milk of magnesia to the skin.*
390. *Dab on some apple cider vinegar. The pinkness and pain will disappear.*
391. *For a super bad burn, put on a paste of water and baking soda.*

Hair shiner
392. *These hair rinses will remove soap film and shine hair: For blondes, rinse water containing a few tablespoons of lemon juice. For brunettes*
and redheads, a few tablespoons of apple cider vinegar in the rinse water.

Broken lipstick
393. *Hold a match under the broken ends until they melt enough to adhere to each other. Cool in the refrigerator.*

Nail polish
394. *Don't throw away that gummy nail polish. Place the bottle in boiling water to bring it back to its original consistency.*
395. *Instead of storing the nail polish bottle right-side-up, put it on its side. Stir it up with the brush when you need some.*
396. *Before you put on polish, put vinegar on your nails. It will clean them completely and help nail polish stick longer.*

Deodorant
397. *To make your own pump-spray deodorant, just add 4 tablespoons of alum to 1 quart of water. Mix it up and put into a spray bottle. If you want a scent, add your favorite cologne.*

Your own manicure
398. *Soak your hands in warm water with lemon juice added. Take them out after about 8 minutes. Rub some lemon peel over the nails while you gently push back the cuticle. Then buff with a soft cloth.*

Baking soda for teeth
399. *Baking soda instead of toothpaste does as good a job. It also works on dentures.*

Cleaning combs and brushes
400. *A solution of baking soda and hot water cleans hair brushes and combs.*

Hair conditioner
401. *Mayonnaise gives dry hair a good conditioning. Apply ½ cup mayonnaise to dry, unwashed hair. Cover with plastic bag and wait for 15 minutes. Rinse a few times be-*

fore shampooing thoroughly.

Homemade dry shampoo
402. Mix together 1 tablespoon salt and ½ cup cornmeal for your own homemade dry shampoo. Transfer to a larger-holed shaker, sprinkle it on oily hair lightly and brush out dirt and grime.

403. Baby powder or cornstarch can also be used as dry shampoos.

Tired eyes
404. Place fresh cold cucumber slices on your eyelids to rid them of redness and puffiness.

*   *   *   *   *   *

X. SEWING

Threading needles
405. Apply some hair spray to your finger and to the end of the thread, stiffening it enough to be easily threaded.

Sharp machine needles
406. Sharpen sewing machine needles by stitching through sandpaper.

Buttons
407. Coat the center of buttons with clear nail polish and they'll stay on longer.

408. On a four-hole button, sew through two holes at a time, knotting the thread and tying off for each set of holes.

409. Use dental floss or elastic thread to sew buttons on children's clothing. The buttons will take a lot of wear before falling off.

Dropped needles and pins
410. Instead of groping around your floor for fallen needles and pins, keep a magnet in your sewing kit. Simply sweep it across your rug to pick up those strays.

Sewing machine oil
411. Stitch through a blotter after oiling your sewing machine to prevent extra oil from damaging your garments.

Patterns
412. Instead of trying to fit used patterns back into their envelopes, store them in plastic bags.

413. Keep patterns from tearing and wrinkle-free by spraying with spray starch.

Recycled elastic
414. Remove elastic waistband from used pantyhose for use in other sewing projects.

Heavy seams
415. Rub seams with a bar of soap to allow a sewing machine needle to easily pass through.

Sewing on nylon
416. When repairing seams on nylon jackets or lingerie, make the job a lot simpler by placing a piece of paper underneath the section you are going to sew. Stitch through the fabric and paper. When finished, tear the paper off.

Order Blank For "Really" Quick and Easy
A Collection of Delicious-Easy-To-Prepare Recipes
From The Ohio Fairfield County
c/o Shirley Heston
4435 Old Logan Road
Lancaster, OH 43130

Please send _____ copies of your cookbook at $10.00 per copy. I have

included $2.00 per copy for postage and handling. Enclosed is my check or

money order for $_____ .

Name: _____

Address: _____

City, State, Zip: _____

Order Blank For "Cookin' in Fairfield County Cookbook"
From the Kitchen of Shirley Heston
c/o Shirley Heston
4435 Old Logan Road
Lancaster, OH 43130

Please send _____ copies of your cookbook at $7.00 per copy. I have

included $3.00 per copy for postage and handling. Enclosed is my check or

money order for $_____ .

Name: _____

Address: _____

City, State, Zip: _____